D0389296

MAR 09 2018

Ballard Branch

START HERE

START HERE

A Road Map to Reducing Mass Incarceration

Greg Berman and Julian Adler

THE NEW PRESS

NEW YORK
LONDON

Requests for permission to reproduce selections from this book should be mailed to: Permissions Department, The New Press, 120 Wall Street, 31st floor, New York, NY 10005.

Published in the United States by The New Press, New York, 2018
Distributed by Two Rivers Distribution

ISBN 978-1-62097-224-3 (e-book)

LIBRARY OF CONGRESS CATALOGING-IN-PUBLICATION DATA

Names: Berman, Greg, author. | Adler, Julian, author.
Title: Start here : a road map to reducing mass incarceration / Greg Berman
    and Julian Adler.
Description: New York : The New Press, [2018] | Includes bibliographical references.
Identifiers: LCCN 2017043125 | ISBN 9781620972236 (hc : alk. paper)
Subjects: LCSH: Prisons—Law and legislation—United States. | Imprisonment—
    United States. | Correctional law—United States. | Criminal justice,
    Administration of—United States. | Law reform—United States.
Classification: LCC KF9730 .B47 2018 | DDC 364.60973—dc23 LC record
    available at https://lccn.loc.gov/2017043125

The New Press publishes books that promote and enrich public discussion and understanding of the issues vital to our democracy and to a more equitable world. These books are made possible by the enthusiasm of our readers; the support of a committed group of donors, large and small; the collaboration of our many partners in the independent media and the not-for-profit sector; booksellers, who often hand-sell New Press books; librarians; and above all by our authors.

www.thenewpress.com

Composition by dix!
This book was set in Bembo

Printed in the United States of America

10 9 8 7 6 5 4 3 2 1

For Alfred Siegel (1951–2014)
Friend, colleague, inspiration

CONTENTS

START HERE

INTRODUCTION

Sometimes the message is delivered by thousands of voices on the streets shouting "black lives matter."

Sometimes the message is found within the pages of carefully argued books like *Locking Up Our Own* or *Race to Incarcerate* that describe the evolution of criminal justice policy in the United States.

And sometimes the message is conveyed through numbers by conservative policymakers decrying the taxpayer dollars that are spent on prisons.

Whether presented in moral, historical, or fiscal terms, the underlying message is the same: the United States locks up too many people.

Roughly 2.3 million people are currently incarcerated in American jails and prisons—a 500 percent increase over the past forty years. It costs an estimated $80 billion a year to keep this machine going.[1] But the human costs are much greater. It is difficult to convey the hardships caused by incarceration in statistics. But it is fair to say that spending time in a county jail or state prison or federal penitentiary typically has a devastating impact on inmates and their families.

Our correctional facilities are no longer designed with rehabilitation foremost in mind, if they ever were. Many observers have labeled these facilities "warehouses." But the truth is far worse—they are accelerants of human misery. If you are poor or mentally ill or struggling to keep your family together when you enter, the chances are that all of these conditions will be markedly worse when you come out.

The negative effects of incarceration are felt by anyone who spends time behind bars. But people of color bear a special burden, considering the history of racism in the American criminal justice system. Our police and prosecutors and courts have not traditionally provided Americans of color with the same protections that they have afforded other citizens. Indeed, the justice system has often been an instrument of oppression, enforcing discriminatory laws and an unjust social order. For many Americans, our jails and prisons are a potent symbol and a present-day manifestation of a litany of historical wrongs.

But this book is not about describing the problem of incarceration in the United States. We take that as a given. Rather, we seek to spell out what is to be done. Instead of decrying the status quo, we want to articulate an affirmative vision of how to reform the American justice system.

We have dedicated our professional lives to this task. We both work for a nonprofit agency, the Center for Court Innovation, that has created a broad range of alternative-to-incarceration and crime prevention programs in the New York area. These programs engage a wide variety of participants, from adults who have committed serious felonies to young people who have engaged in minor rule-breaking. At the Center for Court Innovation, our goal is to show that, contrary to conventional wisdom, it is possible to reduce both crime and incarceration at the same time.

Over the years, we have seen many remarkable transformations. Sullen teens, parolees with lengthy rap sheets, individuals with histories of trauma and victimization . . . these populations (and many more besides) can move from criminality to law-abiding behavior if they are given the right support.

How can these kinds of success stories become the norm rather than the exception? In this book, we attempt to answer this question. We begin where many books about criminal justice end: with solutions.

In the pages that follow, we outline changes to business as usual that we believe can have a significant impact on justice in America—enhancing the fairness of the system, improving the lives of thousands of defendants, and altering the trajectories of crime-plagued communities. We are not utopians. We focus on concrete, ground-level improvements that do not require fundamental changes in the structure of our society. These are real-life reforms that state and local policymakers and practitioners can make in the here and now to reduce our reliance on incarceration.

The good news is that there are dozens of good ideas to choose from. In recent times, innovators have advanced a number of potentially impactful strategies, including changing arrest practices, speeding criminal court case processing, and training criminal justice officials to recognize implicit bias. These, and other ideas, are worth pursuing. But we have chosen to focus on three broad investments that we believe are essential if the justice system is going to live up to its highest ideals in terms of both fairness and effectiveness:

ENGAGE THE PUBLIC IN PREVENTING CRIME.

Our safest neighborhoods, whether rich or poor, do not feel like police states, with officers lurking on every corner. As Jane Jacobs articulated more than fifty years ago in *The Death and Life of Great American Cities*, a crucial element of neighborhood safety is the availability of responsible "eyes on the street," and the willingness of neighbors to enforce social norms and address conditions of disorder. More recently, Robert Sampson of Harvard University has documented the importance of what he labels "collective efficacy"—essentially, a neighborhood's social infrastructure and capacity for joint action on its own behalf, including monitoring and managing the behavior of those who break the rules.

Yet, as currently constructed, the American criminal justice system does precious little to encourage collective efficacy or social cohesion in high-crime neighborhoods. Indeed, a great deal of conventional practice, including overaggressive enforcement and incarceration, tends to undermine the very elements that thinkers like Jacobs and Sampson have identified as crucial to healthy neighborhoods.

How can the justice system help produce safety without relying on traditional strategies—arrest, prosecution, and incarceration—that can, over time, undermine the health of a community? This is a crucial question in the fight against incarceration. Safer neighborhoods mean less crime. Less crime means fewer court cases. And fewer court cases means fewer people sent to jail or prison.

We believe that, if the justice system hopes to reduce victimization and help produce safer neighborhoods, it cannot simply react after crime occurs—it must make a deep investment in crime prevention. And it must reach out to community residents to engage them in the process.

This means participating in campaigns to combat street-level gun violence. This means investing in youth development programs so that teens have pathways to pro-social activities, educational supports, and career opportunities. And this means addressing visible conditions of disorder and reinvigorating public spaces by enhancing visibility and creating programming that brings people out of their buildings to participate in the public square.

As we will show in the pages that follow, these kinds of grassroots efforts are not possible without the people who live and work in our neighborhoods. Criminal justice agencies—not just police, but prosecutors and probation and defense agencies and the courts as well—need to involve local voices in identifying local issues, setting local priorities, and crafting local solutions. And they need to earn the trust of skeptical communities by listening attentively and creating interventions that are designed to address the unique needs and concerns of their target neighborhoods.

TREAT ALL DEFENDANTS WITH DIGNITY AND RESPECT.

A few years ago, researchers from the National Center for State Courts came to evaluate a project of ours in Brooklyn— the Red Hook Community Justice Center. What they found surprised them.

At Red Hook, defendants who have committed misdemeanor offenses are sentenced to perform community service or participate in social service groups for a few days, as an alternative to fines or a short stay in jail. The researchers thought this kind of approach to sentencing was a good thing. They anticipated that it would reduce the use of incarceration and improve conditions in the neighborhood. But they cautioned us that it was highly unlikely that these kinds of short-term interventions would make any difference at all to defendants' lives.

When the evaluators looked at the data, however, comparing participants in the Red Hook program to similar defendants whose cases had received conventional sentences, they discovered that, over the course of three years, the Red Hook defendants had lower re-arrest rates. How was this possible?

The researchers concluded that the answer was simple: Red Hook managed to improve the behavior of participants because it changed the way they felt about the justice system.

From its well-lit entrance with specially trained court officers to its holding cells with specially treated glass instead of bars, the Justice Center in Red Hook is designed to be a user-friendly building that communicates respect for all who pass through its doors. This extends to the courtroom, where Judge Alex Calabrese speaks to defendants using plain language and goes out of his way to give them a chance to tell their side of the story. In Red Hook, all of these small improvements in the atmospherics of the court experience added up to something major: improved compliance with the law.

As it turns out, Red Hook is the living embodiment of an idea known as "procedural justice." Initially expounded by Yale law professor Tom Tyler, the basic concept of procedural justice is straightforward: people do not comply with authorities if they do not believe those authorities to be legitimate. So if you want to encourage law-abiding behavior, it is essential to improve the way that the public (and defendants in particular) perceive the justice system.

At first glance, this might seem a daunting challenge, given how badly the image of justice in this country has been tarnished over the past few years. But we believe that by tweaking the way that police officers, judges, and other criminal justice officials interact with the public, it is possible to improve trust in justice. This means moving from a factory model, where cases are processed like so many widgets, to a customer service orientation that recognizes the fundamental dignity of each individual who comes into contact with the justice system.

In the chapters that follow, we will tell the stories of criminal justice reformers who are trying to reorient the justice system in a way that communicates respect for the public. We will also highlight programs that go a step further, attempting to bring, for lack of a better expression, a dose of love into the lives of defendants. In our experience, the best way to change the behavior of defendants is by creating caring relationships with social workers, judges, mentors, clergy, family members, employers, and others. Almost no one transforms their life without positive connections with their fellow human beings.

LINK PEOPLE TO EFFECTIVE, COMMUNITY-BASED INTERVENTIONS RATHER THAN JAIL OR PRISON.

Many prosecutors and judges, if you can catch them in an unguarded moment, will admit that they do not like sending people to jail or prison. And many defense attorneys will acknowledge that they don't enjoy seeing the same clients with the same problems—addiction, mental illness, unemployment, family dysfunction—return to court over and over again accused of new crimes. A common complaint from criminal justice officials is that they simply lack good options; since they do not have alternatives that they trust, they default to incarceration. If we are to reduce the use of jails and prisons in this country, we must take these concerns seriously.

In recent years, a number of community-based interventions have been documented to change the behavior of offenders. These include programs that link addicted defendants to judicially monitored drug treatment, targeted therapies that seek to alter self-defeating patterns of thought and behavior, and community-focused courts that use community restitution and social services instead of short-term jail sentences and fines.

Over the last generation, we have also learned a lot about how to assess individual defendants' risk of re-offending. There is no longer a need for criminal justice officials—be they probation officers, prosecutors, or judges—to make decisions based primarily on their gut instincts about who should be detained and who should be set free.

Research suggests that very few individuals are immediate threats to public safety. And dozens of effective interventions can be employed at various points in the process to divert defendants from arrest, prosecution, and sentencing. In the pages that follow, we will describe some of the community-based programs that have been documented to reduce re-offending. And we will look at how defendants can be matched to this programming based on the levels of risk they pose to public safety.

We believe that greater investments in both risk assessment and alternative-to-incarceration programs will dramatically improve both the fairness and the effectiveness of our justice system. But in making this case, we are mindful of the dangers of overselling. As Jim Manzi, author of *Uncontrolled: The Surprising Payoff of Trial-and-Error for Business, Politics, and Society* argues, "There is no magic. Those rare programs that do work usually lead to improvements that are quite modest, compared with the size of the problems they are meant to address or the dreams of advocates."[2]

Yet the modestly positive results of alternative programs must always be compared to the abject failures of our jails and prisons. This point is crucial. The success of community-based programs must be judged against the results achieved by incarceration, which is not only expensive but often literally counterproductive, creating more hardened criminals out of low-risk offenders. Moreover, since every inmate is part of a constellation of family members and friends, the ripple effects of reducing incarceration can be profound, altering the future of entire communities.

★   ★   ★

Our vision of criminal justice reform is based on equal parts pragmatism and idealism.

On the one hand, we believe that the state has a legitimate interest in changing the behavior of those who harm the vulnerable and undermine the safety of our neighborhoods. While the Innocence Project and others have pointed out that horrible miscarriages of justice do occur, the truth is that the vast majority of people in our jails and prisons have done something illegal. And this illegal behavior is often quite serious. Many people believe that our prisons are overflowing with the casualties of the War on Drugs—individuals convicted for nonviolent drug offenses. The numbers do not appear to support this argument. As Yale law professor James Forman Jr. writes, "Contrary to the impression left by many of mass incarceration's critics, the majority of America's prisoners are not locked up for drug offenses. . . . Considering all forms of penal institutions together, more prisoners are locked up for violent offenses than for any other type, and just under 25% (550,000) of our nation's 2.3 million prisoners are drug offenders."[3]

At the same time, it is fair to say that most of the people behind bars are not criminal masterminds or psychopaths bent on terrorizing the populace. Instead, they are individuals suffering from trauma, mental illness, substance abuse, unemployment, and substandard education. At the risk of being reductive, there are two ways we can respond to these people: with blame and vindictiveness or with a measure of empathy and kindness.

We believe that, wherever feasible, criminal justice policy should be guided by the better angels of our nature. We are idealistic enough to believe in the human capacity for change, particularly if people are given the proper supports and encouragement. Indeed, we've seen it happen over and over again—addicts getting clean, delinquent young people reengaging in school, and gang members becoming advocates for nonviolent conflict resolution. These kinds of stories are what inspired us to write this book.

More practically, we also know that aside from the tiny minority who die in custody, almost every inmate of our county jails and state and federal prisons eventually returns to life in the community. Whether we want to admit it or not, people with criminal histories are all around us. They are our neighbors. They work with us. They go to the same churches, parks, and stadiums that we do.

As Ta-Nehisi Coates and others have argued, the specter of black criminality has helped to fuel the growth of incarceration in this country by enabling elected officials and the voting public to see criminals as a racialized other. It may be comforting to draw bright lines between "us" and "them," between the law-abiding public and criminals. But in truth, the lines are so blurry as to be nearly nonexistent.

Ironically, the American overuse of incarceration may contain the seeds of its own destruction. There is some evidence to suggest that having gay friends or working alongside those who have recently come to our shores tends to liberalize people's views on social issues like marriage equality and immigration. The fact that so many of us now know someone who has been incarcerated may thus help undermine the public appetite for punitive sentencing in the days to come.

Undoing America's overreliance on incarceration will be difficult. It took us years to get into this mess, and we should expect that it will take us years to get out of it. But we believe that it can be done. James Forman Jr. has reached a similar conclusion. In *Locking Up Our Own*, he argues that mass incarceration is "the result of a series of small decisions, made over time, by a disparate group of actors. If that is correct, mass incarceration will likely have to be undone in the same way." [4]

In this book, we attempt to craft a realistic blueprint for reformers who want to reduce our country's reliance on incarceration, with all of its attendant harms and costs. We begin by asking a simple question: Who is incarcerated in the United States? Understanding who is behind bars—including the seriousness of their offenses, their social service needs, and their demographic characteristics—is an essential first step toward figuring out how to change things.

In chapter 2, we turn to the challenge of community engagement and crime prevention, exploring how criminal justice reformers are reaching out to local residents in creative ways. We use as a case study the work our agency is doing in several neighborhoods in Brooklyn, New York, with high rates of crime and public disenchantment with the justice system.

In chapter 3, we focus on procedural justice, examining how a judge in Newark, New Jersey, is going out of her way to treat defendants with dignity and respect as a means of improving their court experience and their compliance with court mandates.

In chapter 4, we argue that the criminal justice system needs to make greater use of social science and, in particular, the latest advances in assessing the risks and needs presented by defendants. While this approach has its critics, we believe that the careful, transparent, and judicious use of risk assessment offers our best hope for changing the status quo and encouraging decision-makers to reduce their reliance on jail and prison.

The next three chapters address the challenges posed by distinct incarcerated populations. In chapter 5, we consider the need to reduce the number of Americans who are held in jail while their cases are pending in criminal court. We focus in particular on the strides that New York City has made in recent years to reduce pretrial detention, culminating with Mayor Bill de Blasio's historic decision to support closing the city's jail complex on Rikers Island. Chapter 6 examines how the justice system might respond more effectively to addicted defendants, highlighting programs that have succeeded in promoting sobriety. Chapter 7 looks at some of the most vexing problems for reformers—cases involving those who have committed felony offenses. We describe a few of the interventions that have demonstrated success with these populations, including programs that work with mentally ill defendants, troubled young people, and those accused of domestic violence.

Finally, in chapter 8, we take a look at a few states that have sought to change their approach to incarceration, including Utah, Mississippi, and Georgia. Our goal here is to suggest that reducing incarceration is not just a cause for bleeding-heart liberals—even places with strong conservative traditions have taken up the call for change.

We are living through a unique moment, in which it may

be possible to achieve significant reform of our justice system. On the left, activists have highlighted issues of fundamental fairness, including the history of mistreatment that people of color have suffered at the hands of police, prosecutors, judges, and other criminal justice officials. Notwithstanding the law-and-order rhetoric of President Donald Trump, many conservative politicians have also begun to ask questions about the amount of money that is devoted to building and maintaining jails and prisons. And everyone is united in their desire to see crime continue to go down.

Underlying all of the political interest in criminal justice reform is the reality that, despite spikes in selected cities, the rate of violent crime in the United States is low—we have returned to levels of public safety not seen since the 1960s. This may be a time when the public is able to think more clearly about criminal justice policy, rather than embracing demagogic calls to fear.

How long this moment will last is anyone's guess. A 2015 poll commissioned by *Vox* suggests that public support for criminal justice reform may not be terribly deep. The survey of more than two thousand registered voters documented fairly broad agreement that too many people are behind bars in the United States. There was also broad interest in reducing prison sentences for nonviolent drug offenders. But the numbers flipped as soon as the survey asked about changing practice for those who have committed violent offenses; the majority of respondents did not support reducing these sentences.[5]

Many observers worry that rising crime rates could quickly dispel the momentum for reform. "Amnesia about the effect of crime on middle-class voters is a dangerous narcotic," writes Adam Gopnik in *The New Yorker*. "It was crime and the fear of violence, however paranoid or overstated, that impelled the rise of Richard Nixon, and of George Wallace." [6]

In addition to the backlash that a rise in crime might engender, there is the reality of contemporary politics in the United States. It is enormously difficult to get things done, particularly at the federal level. Dozens, if not hundreds, of other compelling issues compete for the attention of policymakers and editorial writers. We have already seen, in the aftermath of Donald Trump's election, that many other fires need to be extinguished.

In short, the window of opportunity for criminal justice reform may not stay open for long. In his "I Have a Dream" speech, Martin Luther King Jr. talked about the "fierce urgency of now." This is certainly a moment of urgency when it comes to criminal justice in this country. The time for diagnosis has passed. Now is the moment for deciding what is to be done. And doing it.

1

WHO IS BEHIND BARS?

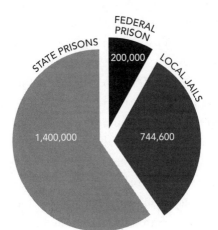

2.3 million Americans are behind bars: approximately **1.4 million** people are serving time in state prisons, **744,600** in local jails, and **200,000** in federal prison[1]

In his 2015 State of the Union address, President Barack Obama issued a bipartisan call for criminal justice reform: "Surely we can agree it's a good thing that for the first time in 40 years, the crime rate and the incarceration rate have come down together, and use that as a starting point for Democrats and Republicans, community leaders and law enforcement, to reform America's criminal justice system so that it protects and serves us all." As President Obama highlighted, in recent years, the rate of incarceration has actually begun to decline in the United States. That's good news, of course. But, according to criminal justice expert Michael Jacobson, this doesn't mean that we are on a path to ending mass incarceration.

Jacobson knows the challenges of incarceration reduction firsthand—back in the 1990s, he served as New York City's corrections commissioner, overseeing the city's jails at a time when there were twenty thousand inmates on Rikers Island on any given day.[2] Today he analyzes jail populations as part of his work at the Institute for State and Local Governance at the City University of New York.

According to Jacobson, turning back the clock to the 1970s, when America incarcerated its citizens at a rate that was similar to the rest of the world's developed countries, would take about one hundred years if we continue on our current trajectory.[3] In his accounting, even the goal of cutting the incarcerated population by 50 percent—the stated target of the reform coalition #cut50—wouldn't get it done. "That does not end mass incarceration," argues Jacobson. "Our rates would still far exceed all other comparisons."

The problem? Violent offenders. They're a perilous third rail for policymakers, especially elected officials who remember how the specter of Willie Horton helped to derail Michael Dukakis's presidential ambitions.

Many reformers prefer to obscure this reality, focusing

on miscarriages of justice or minor drug offenders who are languishing behind bars. But if we're serious about changing course, it will require reckoning with how we understand the mission of our justice system and how we view our fellow citizens who have committed acts of violence at one point or another. "We are such an outlier in how we treat those folks," Jacobson observes. "We have no discussion of human dignity or redemption."

Ending the overuse of incarceration in the United States is possible. But it is not possible unless we take a close and honest look at who is currently behind bars.

"THIS IS NOT ABOUT WHAT THE PRESIDENT DOES"

The United States locks up more of its citizens than any other country on earth. There are more people behind bars in the United States than the incarcerated populations in India and China combined. On a per capita basis, this amounts to incarcerating eight times as many people as Germany, five times as many as Australia, and more than twice as many as Iran.[4]

The incarceration rate in the United States is around 700 inmates per 100,000 people—about one out of every 140 people. But an even starker picture emerges if you consider the incarceration rate for adults. Nationally, one in 100 Americans eighteen years and older is behind bars.[5]

Rates of incarceration vary significantly by region and state.[6] They are highest in the South, but Maine, which has the lowest incarceration rate in the United States, still has an incarceration rate double that of the United Kingdom.[7] Norway has an incarcerated population of about 3,000 compared to Los Angeles's 50,000, despite having a similar number of residents.[8]

The total incarcerated population is approximately 90 percent male.[9] As has been well documented, people of color are overrepresented in prisons and jails. The prison population is 36 percent black and 22 percent Hispanic, compared to a national population that is 13 percent black and 17 percent Hispanic.[10]

All told, close to 2.3 million Americans are incarcerated, which is up from 500,000 in 1980.[11] (Our population has not grown at anywhere near this rate.) These individuals are distributed among the federal prison system, fifty state prison systems, and over three thousand local jail systems.

Although the terms "prison" and "jail" are often used interchangeably, they have specific technical meanings in the context of the American correctional apparatus. Jails, which are operated by cities or counties, typically hold defendants awaiting trial or sentencing, as well as those convicted of crimes that carry a sentence of one year or less. Defendants convicted of more serious crimes are held in prisons, which are run by states or the federal government. In 2014, 744,600 people were serving time in local jails, about 1.4 million people more in state prisons, and about 200,000 more in federal prisons.[12]

While federal reform tends to get most of the attention, the reality is that local jails are significantly busier than both state and federal prisons. In 2014, roughly 11.5 million people were *admitted* to American jails (this includes those people who cycled in and out of jail multiple times during that year). In contrast, fewer than 700,000 inmates were admitted to state and federal prisons combined.[13]

This highlights one of the challenges of incarceration reduction: real reform has to happen at the local level. It is good news that overincarceration has moved from the back burner to the front of the public agenda, discussed by presidential candidates and debated on cable news programs. But there are limits to what can be accomplished at the federal level. If all the federal prisons opened their doors and released all their inmates, the United States would still be the most incarcerated nation in the world.[14]

In *Locking Up Our Own*, James Forman Jr. offers his take on the recent history of criminal justice policy in the United States. In Forman's telling, there is no single identifiable villain responsible for the rise in American incarceration. Instead, he points the finger at dozens of small decisions made at the local level:

When we ask ourselves how America became the world's greatest jailer, it is natural to focus on bright, shiny objects: national campaigns, federal legislation, executive orders from the Oval Office. But we should train our eyes, also, on more mundane decisions and directives, many of which took place at the local level . . .

small choices, made daily, over time, in every corner of our nation, are the bricks that built our prison nation.[15]

Jeremy Travis, former president of the John Jay College of Criminal Justice, concurs. "Ultimately, this is not about what the president does, or even Congress," says Travis. "This is about states and, ultimately, communities."[16] While federal officials like President Obama have tried to change the national conversation, to effect real change means going county by county to change the practice (and, hopefully, the hearts and minds) of local politicians, prosecutors, and judges.

BEYOND NONVIOLENT CASES

Many people believe that the vast majority of individuals behind bars are serving time for nonviolent offenses, particularly drug crimes.[17] "America's prisons are dangerously overcrowded, and the War on Drugs is mainly to blame," the *Huffington Post* recently declared.[18] For the federal prison population, this belief is basically accurate—about half of federal inmates are nonviolent drug offenders.[19] But this population still accounts for just a sliver of the incarcerated population nationwide—less than 5 percent.[20]

At the state level, the data tell a different story. The majority of inmates in state prisons (53.2 percent) have a violent offense listed as their primary charge. Only 16 percent of those in state prison are serving time for nonviolent drug crimes.[21]

Put simply, we cannot solve our overincarceration problem

just by changing the way we treat nonviolent drug offenders. Make no mistake: there are still many drug offenders behind bars, and we should be working assiduously to figure out a better way to respond to drug crime. But this alone will not solve the problem of incarceration in the United States.

In recent years, numerous theories have been advanced to explain the massive increase in the American incarcerated population. Certainly, it is possible to make the case that rising crime rates in the 1980s helped fuel the growth in American prisons. But viewed in aggregate, crime rates in the United States have been declining for a quarter century. Why has the incarcerated population continued to expand?

The answer, according to Fordham University law professor John Pfaff, is pretty straightforward: blame the prosecutors. Across the country, many state legislatures have passed sentencing laws (for example, mandatory minimums, three-strikes-and-you're-out, and truth-in-sentencing reforms) to strengthen penalties for criminal behavior. Whether intended or not, these laws ended up tilting the playing field in the direction of prosecutors, who wield enormous discretion over whether to charge a defendant and for what offense. According to Pfaff,

> The probability that a district attorney files a felony charge against an arrestee goes from about 1 in 3, to 2 in 3. So over the course of the '90s and 2000s, district attorneys just got much more aggressive in how they filed charges. Defendants who they would not have

filed felony charges against before, they now are charging with felonies . . . the number of felony cases filed
shoots up very strongly, even as the number of arrests
goes down . . . the real growth in the prison population
comes from county-level district attorneys sending violent people to prison.[22]

Pfaff focuses on violent people for good reason, but when
you take a closer look at the incarcerated population, it becomes clear that drawing bright lines between violent and
nonviolent offenses isn't so easy. While policymakers often use
"violent offender" as shorthand for someone who poses a clear
threat to public safety and "nonviolent offender" as someone
who does not, the reality is murkier. The population of violent
offenders includes those convicted of crimes like murder and
sexual assault, but it also includes those convicted of simple assault, which may not involve any physical harm to the victim.
(Shoving someone during an argument could be charged as a
simple assault, for example.)[23] The violent crime of robbery,
the top charge for 180,000 state prisoners, is defined rather ex-
pansively as "the completed or attempted theft, directly from a
person, of property or cash by force or threat of force, with or
without a weapon, and with or without injury."[24]

Even murder has its gray areas. Consider the felony murder
rule, which exists in some form in forty-six states and in the
federal penal code.[25] This rule enables prosecutors to charge

with murder an individual who has committed or facilitated a felony that resulted in a person's death, even if the individual had no direct involvement in the death.[26] For example, in a 2004 case that attracted national attention, a Florida man named Ryan Holle was charged with first-degree murder because a car he had lent a friend was used in a burglary that resulted in the killing of a young woman. The prosecutor successfully argued that under Florida's felony murder rules, Holle, who had no previous criminal record and was not present at the scene of the crime, was as culpable for the woman's death as the burglars themselves. Holle was convicted and sentenced to life in prison without the possibility of parole.[27]

Of course, nonviolent crime can be complicated too. Offenders classified as nonviolent often have violent histories. A charge like weapons possession, for which more than 50,000 people are currently incarcerated in state prison, is classified by the federal government as a nonviolent public order crime. Driving under the influence, the top charge for 25,000 state prisoners, receives the same classification. The number of state prison inmates with drug possession listed as their top charge (47,000) is dwarfed by the number with other drug charges (160,500), including trafficking, which is often associated with more serious violent crime.[28] At the end of the day, it is difficult to make clear determinations about who is a threat to public safety based solely on conviction charges.

A HUMAN PERSPECTIVE

Of course, inmates are not just numbers on a page—they are people. And the data suggest that they are people with a host of problems, including serious behavioral health needs.

A comprehensive study by the National Center on Addiction and Substance Abuse at Columbia University found that 85 percent of the incarcerated population in the United States were under the influence of drugs or alcohol at the time of their crime, had a history of substance abuse, committed their offense to get money to buy drugs, were incarcerated for an alcohol- or drug-related offense, or some combination of these characteristics.[29] More worrying, 64.5 percent of incarcerated individuals met the formal criteria for a substance use disorder.[30]

Mental illness is similarly prevalent. According to the Bureau of Justice Statistics, 64 percent of inmates in local jails, 56 percent in state prison, and 45 percent in federal prison struggle with mental health problems.[31]

Histories of trauma and victimization are common among the incarcerated population. More than a quarter of inmates report being abandoned by their parents or guardians during childhood.[32] And 19 percent of inmates report histories of physical or sexual abuse.[33]

Female inmates are particularly vulnerable. The United States is home to only 5 percent of the world's female population yet it accounts for almost 30 percent of the world's incarcerated women.[34] Well over half of the female inmates in state prisons have experienced abuse of one form or another.[35] In fact, 90 percent of female inmates meet the criteria for a lifetime diagnosis of serious mental illness, PTSD, or substance abuse disorder.[36] One 2011 study of state prisoners found rates of post-traumatic stress disorder as high as 40 percent for women, which is comparable to those found among combat veterans.[37] Women held in local jails represent the fastest growing population of incarcerated people in the United States. According to a report from the Vera Institute of Justice and the MacArthur Foundation, "For women, jail can be especially destabilizing because most jail environments were not designed with them in mind and do not take into account the particular adversities they have experienced."[38]

Women are hardly the only incarcerated population with unique needs. Other groups that are ill served by the American correctional apparatus include:

- **Young People:** The United States incarcerates more young people in juvenile detention facilities than any other industrialized country—over 60,000 in 2011. An additional 95,000 young people were incarcerated in adult jails and prisons that same year.[39] Young people between the ages of eighteen and twenty-four make up roughly a quarter of all prison admissions in the United States.[40]
- **The Elderly:** The number of Americans sixty-five years or older serving prison sentences has increased

by 63 percent since 2007. Long sentences mean that many of these older prisoners—whose medical costs are three to nine times higher than those of younger inmates—will be well into their seventies, eighties, or nineties before they are released.[41]

- **LGBTQ:** Lesbian, gay, and bisexual individuals are overrepresented in prisons and jails. According to a 2011 study, 33 percent of women in prison and 26 percent of women in jail identify as lesbian or bisexual. The incarceration rate of self-identified lesbian, gay, or bisexual individuals was 1,882 per 100,000—more than three times that of the U.S. adult population.[42] At this point, there isn't good data to document the numbers of transgender individuals behind bars, but a report from the Center for American Progress argues that transgender individuals have higher rates of incarceration than the general population.[43]

Members of all of these groups who come into jail or prison with personal challenges often leave with these same challenges exacerbated. Experience tells us that without effective interventions, they are liable to make a quick return to jail. Rates of re-incarceration are particularly high among those with mental illness and substance abuse problems.[44]

"Our traditional court system is designed to produce recidivists," concludes Judge Alex Calabrese of Brooklyn, New York. "People appear before me with long records of committing crimes to support their addiction or as a result of mental health issues that have not been adequately addressed. What I find particularly frustrating is that when I ask defendants whether they have ever been in drug or mental health treatment, they typically say no." [45]

Meaningful efforts to reduce incarceration must grapple with this reality—simply releasing people to the streets is not enough. "If we really want to make great strides in reducing incarceration," explains George Mason University criminologist Faye Taxman, "then we have to build up community capacity to help people." [46]

As currently constructed, the American justice system is not designed to build up community capacity or, frankly, to help people. But that doesn't mean that this must always be so. "We chose to be here," says Jeremy Travis. "We can choose not to be here."

2

PLANTING SEEDS

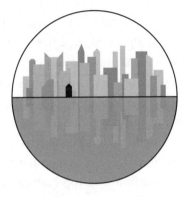

Research suggests that roughly **half** of all crime comes
from just **3 percent** to **6 percent** of a city landscape[1]

Brownsville, Brooklyn, is a community with a well-earned reputation for toughness.

"Never ran, never will" is the unofficial neighborhood motto.[2] The toughness of Brownsville can be seen in some of the neighborhood's favorite sons—hard-core rappers like M.O.P. and boxers like Riddick Bowe and Zab Judah. Brownsville's toughness can also be found in the material conditions of the neighborhood, which is home to eighteen separate public housing developments. It is estimated that 44 percent of the local working-age population is out of the workforce.[3]

Crime is one of the defining features of Brownsville. Brownsville has been called the "murder capital" of New York; the neighborhood recently ranked dead last out of sixty-nine communities, with the highest per capita homicide rate in the city.[4] In 2015, the injury assault rate in Brownsville was the highest in New York City.[5] "There are also a number of unreported crimes," says Viola Greene-Walker, the manager of the local community board. "Street-justice type crimes."[6] In a 2010 survey of local residents conducted by the Center for Court Innovation, 80 percent of respondents identified guns, gangs, drugs, and assault as the top community problems in Brownsville.[7]

Another defining feature of Brownsville is the prevalence of incarceration. In 2015, Brownsville's incarceration rate ranked the second-highest in New York City.[8] According to the Justice Mapping Center, the state of New York spends $40 million a year incarcerating people just from Brownsville.[9] And these numbers don't include the thousands of Brownsville residents who are held at the local jail on Rikers Island.

So Brownsville is a high-crime, high-incarceration community. It is also a community with a history of disenchantment with the justice system. The criminal justice system is not an abstraction in Brownsville—it is a daily fact of life. A juvenile detention facility is located in the community. Thousands of local residents are under probation or parole supervision. And police are a visible presence: an eight-block area of Brownsville had the highest concentration of "stop, question, and frisks" in the city, according to a 2010 *New York Times* report.[10]

It is safe to say that familiarity has not led to fondness. The justice system enjoys depressingly low levels of community support in Brownsville, where more than nine out of ten residents are African American or Latino. For understandable reasons, many of these residents do not believe that the legal system exists to protect them.[11] Twenty-five-year-old Xavier Pittman of Brownsville describes this dynamic: "We police ourselves. I say that to mean when something goes on, the last people to find out is the police. If I have an issue with you, I'm going to handle the issue with you. . . . I'm not going to call the police. That's a waste of my minutes on my phone, that's a waste of my life. All they're going to do is come in and complicate the situation even further."[12] The kind of cynicism about the justice system that exists in Brownsville is corrosive. At its most extreme, it breeds criminal behavior—if the laws don't exist to serve people like me, why should I obey them?

Brownsville is, of course, a unique place with its own particular culture and history. But it is also emblematic of many poor neighborhoods with large minority populations. "Our system was never set up with an eye out for racial equity," explains Tshaka Barrows, of the W. Haywood Burns Institute. "We believe that you cannot engage racial and ethnic disparities and do a meaningful job of it without engaging the communities that are directly impacted by those issues." [13] Mark Soler, of the Children's Center for Law and Policy, agrees, adding that the incorporation of community voices "provides urgency": "We have to impress upon the professionals in the system that the world looks very differently from the other side of the desk." [14]

To be fair, the City of New York has been trying for decades to reduce crime in Brownsville. But these efforts have typically relied upon a heavy police presence. For example, Brownsville was one of the neighborhoods that the NYPD selected for its "Operation Impact" initiative, which flooded the community with officers, many of them inexperienced graduates fresh from the police academy. Perhaps predictably, one of the side effects of this program was a lot of negative interactions between police officers and local residents—in the 2010 Brownsville community survey, only 16 percent of local residents characterized their relationship with police as positive.

COMMUNITY-BASED CRIME PREVENTION
What if there were a way to improve public safety in places like Brownsville without emphasizing more and more enforcement?

We started asking this question in 2011 when our agency, the Center for Court Innovation, launched the Brownsville Community Justice Center. The Justice Center seeks to combat crime by engaging local teens in pro-social programming and by addressing neighborhood eyesores and hot spots. Using our work in Brownsville—and similar work we have done in nearby Crown Heights and Bedford-Stuyvesant—as a jumping-off point, this chapter argues that any effort to reduce incarceration must begin with an investment in community-based crime prevention. The logic is straightforward: many people are behind bars for violent crime. If we can reduce this behavior, we will reduce the prison pipeline.

While the logic may be simple enough, the implementation is anything but. James Brodick, who leads the Brownsville Community Justice Center, acknowledges this. "Most so-called community engagement efforts are bullshit," he says.[15] It is not uncommon for a one-off town hall meeting to mark both the beginning and the end of any such effort. "It takes commitment, it takes beyond a nine-to-five," emphasizes Viola Greene-Walker, of the Brownsville community board. "Not everybody is willing to put that forth."

But a commitment to long hours is only the beginning of what is required. Community-based crime prevention efforts must also grapple with the messy dynamics of neighborhood violence.

According to University of Miami law professor Donna Coker, it is often hard to draw bright lines between perpetrators and victims. "Many of the people who are either under the supervision of the criminal justice system or incarcerated are themselves victims of very serious abuse," she says.[16] Indeed, the National Center for Trauma-Informed Care estimates that trauma is a near-universal experience among defendants.[17]

This is certainly the case in New York City. Our organization recently interviewed nearly one thousand people charged with misdemeanors whose cases continued beyond arraignment in the boroughs of Manhattan, Brooklyn, and the Bronx. The prevalence of trauma was staggering: more than half of the sample reported having witnessed a shooting or other violent event. One in four reported having experienced physical, emotional, or sexual abuse. Nearly 20 percent said they had attempted suicide.[18]

The Safe Horizon Counseling Center is an outpatient mental health clinic in Brooklyn that specializes in trauma-informed care. According to Victoria Dexter, defendants referred from court almost always report the same story:

> As young children, they were introduced to self-medication with substances by perpetrators. . . . Their abuse was ongoing, which meant that their nervous systems actually became optimized for responding to danger and not coping and thriving and loving and making art and all these other things that they could have been doing as little kids. Instead, their nervous systems became devoted to scanning and managing danger, and that's exhausting. It's depleting. It's demoralizing.[19]

Anyone can experience trauma, of course. But not all populations experience equal rates of trauma, particularly violent crime. Young people of color are especially vulnerable.

According to Lenore Anderson, of Californians for Safety and Justice, "When we see a young African American male walking down the street, we shouldn't be afraid of him, we should be afraid *for* him."[20]

INTERRUPTING VIOLENCE

Mark's experience is a case in point.[21] A nineteen-year-old African American man from Brooklyn, Mark was charged with a felony-level gun crime in 2016. Although this was his first serious charge, it was not his first brush with violence. In the past, Mark had been on the other side of the gun—the target of multiple shootings.

Following his arrest, Mark was attacked by individuals connected to the victim of the gun crime. He was stabbed multiple times on the subway and left to die. Mark survived and was hospitalized for several days.

After the stabbing, Mark avoided the subway and refused to leave his apartment without a friend present. He had trouble sleeping. He constantly surveyed his surroundings for potential threats. He replayed the attack over and over in his mind. In the space of a few short weeks, Mark had gone from victim to alleged perpetrator and back to victim again.

This story doesn't come as a surprise to the team at Save Our Streets (S.O.S.) Brooklyn, which seeks to end shootings in the neighborhoods of Crown Heights and Bedford-Stuyvesant. S.O.S. Brooklyn treats community violence as a public health problem, seeking to halt the spread of retaliatory violence in the same way that epidemiologists might combat an infectious disease. This idea, which was pioneered by Gary Slutkin and the Cure Violence organization in Chicago, focuses on recruiting "credible messengers"—those who have engaged in violent behavior in the past but have discovered the error of their ways—to spread an anti-violence message to their peers. "The credible messengers are trying to identify, detect, and interrupt the transmission of the violent event," explains Amy Ellenbogen, of S.O.S. Brooklyn. "The most common reason why violence spreads is because violence preceded it." [22]

In Crown Heights and Bedford-Stuyvesant, these "violence interrupters" work evenings and nights to identify and mediate street conflicts before they escalate into violence. Ife Charles, who helps oversee the program, says that the violence interrupters function as "ears to the street," identifying emerging conflicts: "They're in the street with the young people from eleven to two in the morning or four in the morning, whatever time young people hang out. They're in there listening to the rhetoric. Who's boasting, who's got the ego, who's the person that's calling themselves the boss, who's the person that's talking." [23]

In addition to attempting to de-escalate conflict before guns are drawn, S.O.S. staff actively try to recruit troubled young people who want to make significant life changes. "We're trying to stop the shootings and killings, but we're also trying to change the norms in the community," notes Ellenbogen.

Sometimes what kids need is simply a mentor who is willing to listen to them. Sometimes they need help figuring out how to find a job or get enrolled in school. And sometimes they need quite a bit more. When this happens, the S.O.S. team turns to Kenton Kirby.

Kirby runs a program called Make It Happen that attempts to engage young men of color like Mark in individual and group therapy to help them deal with their histories of trauma. That's what Kirby is doing, but that's not how he describes it to most of the participants. "A lot of young black men don't want to be looked at as victims," says Kirby.[24]

How do you sell therapy to people who don't see themselves as needing it? For Kirby, the first step is often to address other issues. "They may not even be ready to talk about the trauma experiences when they don't know where they're going to sleep that night, they don't know where they're going to get their next meal," explains Kirby. "Working on the immediate needs is the priority."[25]

Once Kirby has earned a measure of trust, the next step is to spark a conversation about the nature of masculinity. Participants are challenged to think about how their definition of manhood is intertwined with trauma. "My guys don't really have a space to process complex emotions," Kirby said. "When someone acts out, a lot of times, there is some unrecognized trauma."[26]

This requires a delicate balancing act. According to Kirby: "Many of the young men in our program have described horrific instances of personal victimization. . . . In the 'Make It Happen' program, we do not condone criminal actions, but we also feel that it is important to not lose sight of the pain and compounded trauma our clients have experienced."[27]

Over the course of ten weeks' worth of group workshops and one-on-one counseling sessions, Kirby attempts to guide his clients toward a healthier conception of black masculinity that does not condone violence. According to criminologist Charlotte Gill, of George Mason University, this kind of approach is crucial to effective community-based crime prevention programs. Reviewing the research literature, Gill concluded that programs that target young people and focus on stopping crime at its source tend to be more effective than programs that attempt to supervise, rehabilitate, or deter those who have already offended. Across the board, she identified "the proactive effort to connect the individual to the community on a one-to-one basis" as the key element of a good program's success.[28] According to Gill's analysis, community-based crime prevention initiatives are most effective when they are "highly focused—whether at small places or with high-risk individuals."[29]

Make It Happen and S.O.S. Brooklyn are addressing neighborhood violence in ways that are both direct and immediate. But often community-based crime prevention takes the form of long-term investments that may take years to reap dividends. The Brownsville Community Justice Center is planting these kinds of seeds in central Brooklyn.

"SAVE MY SON"

On an unseasonably warm October morning in 2016, Erica Mateo, of the Brownsville Community Justice Center, is standing in a once-empty lot that will soon be unveiled as the site of a new clubhouse for area young people. The clubhouse is a much-needed addition to a local housing complex notorious for high rates of gun violence and police activity. Mateo and her colleague Deron Johnston are surrounded by young people who are preparing for the start of the ribbon-cutting ceremony. Some are greeting guests. Others are setting up the sound system. Still others are putting food on trays.

The teenagers played a crucial role in the development of the clubhouse, working with L+M Development Partners to design the project from soup to nuts. They placed a large shipping container at the center of the space that could be used for a broad range of classes and activities. Participants also included ample grassy spaces to allow for exercise, gardening, and picnics. In addition to a safe space for after-school activities, the clubhouse will also host community meetings and events, including neighborhood movie nights, holiday celebrations, and musical performances.

The clubhouse is really two projects in one. First, it is a youth development project that seeks to provide participants with concrete skills and opportunities during their after-school hours. But it is also an effort to remake the physical landscape of Brownsville in ways that promote safety.

The need for a safe haven was clear from the start of the

project. Erica Mateo recalls the conversations with young people that led to the decision to create the clubhouse: "Safety came up over and over and over. Safety issues were part of every minute of every day of their lives. Walking down the block, going to the store, they talked about it all the time. They were like, 'We don't leave here because if we do, we feel really unsafe.' Even young people who weren't involved in gangs or gang activity felt the same way: they could not leave their development."[30]

Of course, safety is just one of many problems facing Brownsville. More than half of the children in Brownsville grow up in households below the poverty line. Life expectancy is among the lowest of any place in New York. Many of the services that New Yorkers take for granted—banking, grocery stores, easy access to the subway—are limited or simply nonexistent. According to Apurva Mehrotra, of the Citizens Committee for Children, "What makes Brownsville unique is you have a scarcity of a whole slew of assets. It's not a mild scarcity. I really don't think there are many—or any—other neighborhoods in the city, even those that are economically distressed, that are in that kind of situation."[31]

As Mehrotra makes clear, there are a host of needs in a place like Brownsville, including greater investments in health care, education, and jobs. Improving the physical environment is also crucial. We know from years of research that violence is intimately linked to specific neighborhood contexts.[32] Research suggests that about 50 percent of crime is found in just

3 to 6 percent of a city landscape.[33] Zooming in, about 20 to 25 percent of crime is found at only 1 percent of the places in a city (that is, single blocks or even smaller street segments).[34]

Researchers have documented that a community's environment plays an important role in regulating behavior.[35] Put simply, our physical surroundings can either encourage or discourage crime. Mateo and her colleagues hope that the clubhouse in Brownsville will be a step in the right direction, creating a place where positive things can happen. Mateo, who grew up in Brownsville, also emphasizes the symbolic value of the project: "I come from Brownsville. Brownsville is known as [a place where] we rob people, we shoot people. We're not known as people who go to college . . . or people who use their agencies for good things. The clubhouse is a visual signifier that that's not true."

For James Brodick, who heads up the Brownsville Community Justice Center, this is the ultimate goal of all of the youth development work he and his colleagues are doing: "We're planting seeds. We're trying to invest in the next generation in Brownsville, and give them the tools they need to be effective advocates for themselves and their community." Brodick understands that this is a long-term investment: "I'm not sure that we'll be able to judge the ultimate impact for a decade."

But some of the seeds that Brodick and his colleagues have planted are already bearing fruit.

Not long ago, Erica Mateo got a call from Chris, a

participant in one of the Justice Center's youth programs. Chris let Mateo know that his younger brother had been shot and killed in the Bronx. Just twenty-three years old, Chris was no stranger to tragedy—he had already lost his oldest brother six months earlier.

Mateo and Deron Johnston found Chris drunk on a street corner, surrounded by friends and acquaintances demanding retaliation. Revealing two guns, an acquaintance asked Chris, "Do you want to handle this situation?" If Mateo and Johnston had not been present, who knows how this scenario might have played out. But they were there. And together they were able to bundle Chris in their car and return him safely to Brownsville.

It wasn't luck that led Mateo and Johnston to that street corner on that fateful night for Chris—it was the product of years of work and relationship building. Mateo first met Chris two years earlier when his father brought him to the Brownsville Community Justice Center. Chris had just returned home from Rikers Island. He was facing felony-level assault charges. But like so many other young men of color, Chris was also a victim. He had been shot before, taking two bullets to his hip. Sitting in Mateo's office, Chris's father had pleaded with her to "save my son."

Chris wasn't sure what to make of the program at first. He and the other participants worked on several projects designed to benefit the community, including a neighborhood garden and several large-scale murals. They wore purple T-shirts emblazoned with the Brownsville Community Justice Center logo. "At first, they thought the T-shirts were corny," says Mateo. "But then they went outside, and saw the way people reacted to them, like 'you're doing something dope, you're doing something positive, congratulations.' After that, they started wearing them with pride." Xavier Pittman, who also participated in the program, acknowledged the power of the T-shirt. "I feel deputized," he explains. "I am going to hold up this Brownsville Community Justice Center T-shirt the way I used to hold up my [gang] flag."

Getting at-risk young people to trade gang flags for T-shirts with positive messages on them is, at some level, the goal of most community crime prevention initiatives. According to the Brownsville team, there is no single, magic ingredient to making this happen. Chris's story suggests that it takes a host of ingredients—and a dash of luck—to alter someone's trajectory.

In the case of Chris, these elements included a resource center located in his neighborhood and staffed by extremely dedicated professionals willing to go above and beyond the call of duty for the young people in their charge. Another essential ingredient was patience: it took time to establish a trusting relationship with Chris. The final component was a willingness to engage Chris's entire family. In addition to working with Chris, Mateo and Johnston also provided help to other family members, connecting his mother to mental health services, and his older brother Devon to job training.

47

Chris's story isn't over. It remains to be seen whether he will transform his life. But thanks to the Brownsville Community Justice Center, he managed to avoid the temptation of retaliatory violence and all of the consequences that can follow from a moment of madness. "They helped my family get through tragedy," reflects Chris's brother Devon. "They picked us up—helped us to avoid the downfall." [36] This is the painstaking pathway to a safer Brownsville: one crucial moment, and one vulnerable young person, at a time.

3

TAMING THE GREEN MONSTER

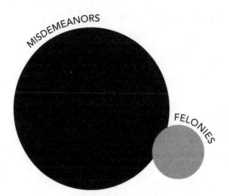

Most criminal cases in the United States are misdemeanors. Misdemeanors outnumber felonies by approximately **3 to 1**[1]

In many places, the local courthouse is a shining architectural jewel, a monument, a place of civic pride. In Newark, New Jersey, the courthouse, which is located on Green Street, is known to local residents as "the Green Monster."

"Newark Municipal Court was probably one of the worst places you wanted to be in," says Randy Burley, from the nearby New Hope Baptist Church soup kitchen.[2] "You got no respect from the judges, from the officers. The Monster's a horrible place."

The conditions at the Green Street jail facility, where arrestees are held before seeing a judge, are a big part of the problem. "I mean, you didn't want to get locked up there," says Burley, "because the bathroom was flooded, it smelled like vomit . . . and urine, and you'd be in a cell with a person that's dope sick, going through problems, and the police just didn't care."

"They say it's a horrible, horrible place to go to," echoes Sr. Pastor Felicia R. Osborne, of Newark's Bethel Family & Youth Resource Center. "They say there's [bed] bugs, and it's just very unpleasant."[3] After a rash of suicides in 2014, the U.S. Department of Justice found grave reason for concern:

> The [Newark Police Department] provides no special or additional training to officers who are assigned to the holding facility, and some officers report that assignment to the holding facility is undesirable, and commonly perceived as an informal punishment. The layout of the Cell Block offers only limited lines of sight into the cells, and the cells all contain suicide hazards such as exposed crossbars which could be used as hanging points.[4]

Each year, the Green Monster consumes thousands of people—in a city of over 280,000 residents, the Newark

Municipal Court hears about 42,000 cases annually involving minor drug possession, property crimes, and other low-level offenses.[5]

Like many places, Newark provides judges with limited options when it comes to dealing with these kinds of crimes. Often, the choices boil down to this: jail or fines.

While at first glance, a fine might appear preferable to time behind bars, the two outcomes may not be as different as you think. Given the financial realities of many defendants, fines often go unpaid. And unpaid fines lead to warrants. And arrest warrants lead to jail.

"There was a very long line of people just getting arrested primarily because they were poor and they couldn't pay their bill to the City of Newark," recalls public defender Ashlie Gibbons.[6] Municipal Court data from 2007 to 2008 show that nine out of ten defendants were sentenced to pay fines, with an average fine amount of $175.[7] Gibbons describes clients who were forced to choose between paying fees and fines and making ends meet: "Many just threw their hands up and said, 'I can't pay and I don't know what to do.'"

This is a daily fact of life in the Green Monster. Judge Victoria Pratt explains the view from the bench in a case where the prosecutor suggested a fine of $50: "One day there was a defendant in court who had on one shoe, and I said, 'Fifty dollars? Madam Prosecutor, didn't you notice that he's got on one shoe.' Now he can't pay fifty dollars. This doesn't even make sense. It's my job as the judge to ensure that the interests of justice are met. It doesn't serve the interest of justice to give somebody a fine they can't pay and not give them a way to pay it."

The frontline practitioners in Newark are not the only ones who have noted the absurdity of this situation—during Barack Obama's administration, the U.S. Department of Justice took notice as well.[8] In announcing an initiative to rethink the use of fees and fines, Attorney General Loretta E. Lynch emphasized that "[t]he consequences of the criminalization of poverty are not only harmful—they are far-reaching." According to Lynch, incarcerating individuals who cannot afford to pay fees and fines "contribute[s] to an erosion of our faith in government."[9]

Alexandra Natapoff, a professor at Loyola Law School in Los Angeles and a leading authority on misdemeanor crime, describes how the widespread use of fees and fines can ultimately result in disparate punishments: "A wealthy person can pay a fifty-dollar, hundred-dollar, two-hundred-dollar, three-hundred-dollar fine and exit the system and get out of that dysfunctional dance with probation officers and courts and court dates. Poor people don't have that option. In effect, we are ensuring that poor people will suffer more from a misdemeanor experience than wealthy people will precisely because we rely so heavily on fines and fees."[10]

OFFERING ALTERNATIVES

In 2011, Newark Community Solutions was created to offer alternatives to jail and fines for misdemeanors and other
minor offenses in Newark Municipal Court.[11] "This program
is about ending cycles of recidivism," said then mayor Cory
Booker.[12] "Very pragmatically, I'm hoping this helps us . . .
restore more faith in the justice system locally."[13] The project seeks to reduce the use of both incarceration and fines by
promoting community service and social service mandates in
their stead. Services range from job training and educational
assistance to drug and mental health treatment.

Nearly a quarter of the defendants enrolled in Newark
Community Solutions arrive with active bench warrants for
failure to pay fines.[14] "The number may even be higher," notes
project director Kelly Mulligan-Brown. "Often, defendants
initially appear in court on a new charge, and only later do
we find out that they actually have old fines owed as well."[15]
By successfully completing community service and social services, defendants are able to simultaneously resolve both new
charges and old fines—thereby leaving the program without
criminal justice debt.

Public defender Ashlie Gibbons thinks Newark Community Solutions has changed the dynamic in the Newark Municipal Court: "Now when individuals get arrested and they're
in the holding cell, they say, 'Mr. Gibbons, can you see if you
can get me in the Newark Community Solutions program?
I've got to get this behind me. I want to make something of

my life, but I don't have the present financial ability to do that. But if you will help me with my fines, then I can go out and get my license and get other parts of my life together.'" As Gibbons makes clear, Newark Community Solutions is serving a population that would otherwise cycle in and out of jail. It is a population with serious problems: Judge Pratt estimates that 85 to 90 percent of the defendants she sees have substance abuse problems, and that more than 40 percent have mental health needs.[16]

Darryl is an example of a Newark Community Solutions client trying to get his life together. Darryl was only twenty-five years old, but he already had a criminal record and several open cases when he appeared before Judge Pratt on a charge of drug possession. He was mandated to perform community service cleaning the streets and serving food at a local soup kitchen. In addition, Darryl participated in several individual counseling sessions with a case manager. During these sessions, Darryl shared that he was taking classes to prepare for his GED. He reported that he had previously taken the exam and passed all but a few sections. His case manager collaborated with a community-based GED program to assist Darryl with his studies. Two months after successfully completing his court obligations and pleading guilty to a lesser charge, Darryl walked into the courthouse to inform the judge and his case manager that he had passed the test. He is currently enrolled at a local community college.[17]

Darryl's story is a case study of how a criminal case can

be viewed as a window of opportunity to help defendants get their lives on track. Another case in point is Isabelle, age twenty-one, who also came to the Newark Municipal Court charged with drug possession. Rather than sentence her to jail or impose a fine, Judge Pratt mandated Isabelle to five days of social service and two days of community service. During an intake interview, Isabelle disclosed that she was addicted to heroin. Her Newark Community Solutions case manager referred her to a voluntary treatment program. Thanks to her progress in the program, Isabelle's case was ultimately dismissed. Two years after her initial appearance before Judge Pratt, Isabelle is now drug free. She is enrolled in cosmetology school and has had no further contact with the justice system.[18]

Darryl and Isabelle are just two of the hundreds of cases that Newark Community Solutions handles each year. Alexandra Natapoff, of Loyola Law School, explains the broader significance of what is happening in Newark:

> The Department of Justice report on Ferguson I think put the pieces of the puzzle together for people in a way that they had not previously understood. They [now] understood that the criminal system's regressive tax on poor people, and the racial disproportion in imposing that tax, is part and parcel of the failure of the lower-level courts; that it generates tension and conflict between the [system actors] and the low-income communities who they police and also from whom they

are extracting revenue. Those things are inextricably intertwined in the misdemeanor system in a way we miss when we talk about mass incarceration [and only focus on] serious felonies.

As Natapoff makes clear, much of the public conversation about crime in our country tends to focus on felony-level defendants. But to ignore misdemeanors is to ignore the majority of people in the criminal justice system. An estimated 10 million misdemeanor cases are filed annually.[19] Although it is hard to locate many conclusive statistics on the number of individuals behind bars for misdemeanors, according to the most recent data available nearly 75 percent of the local jail population in the United States is behind bars for nonviolent traffic, property, drug, or public order offenses.[20]

In recent years, some criminal justice policymakers have begun to question the wisdom of business as usual in misdemeanor cases. For example, the late Brooklyn District Attorney Ken Thompson decided not to prosecute individuals who were arrested for possessing less than 25 grams (just under an ounce) of marijuana.[21] And in many cities, police departments, under pressure from protestors, have begun to rethink "broken windows" policing, with its emphasis on aggressive low-level law enforcement.

At the same time, it is also true that many communities actively argue on behalf of quality-of-life law enforcement, looking to the justice system to address disorderly conduct, street prostitution, and other visible signs of lawlessness. How can the justice system take these concerns seriously without jailing more people? What should judges do when they are confronted with thousands of misdemeanor cases?

PROCEDURAL JUSTICE

For Judge Pratt in Newark, there are two answers. The first we have already discussed: drastically reducing the use of jail and fines and using community restitution and social services instead. But Pratt believes that this alone is not enough; she thinks that judges should also change the way that they interact with defendants. She is particularly focused on communicating with each defendant clearly:

> I start with "good morning sir/ma'am, please state your name for the record," and if I can't hear them—if they whisper—I'll just say, "I can't hear you. Can you please just say that again?" I smile when I'm talking to them, and I ask them how they are feeling and actually wait for a response. I try to make them feel comfortable in the short period of time that we have, while also getting down to business. Listening to how they say their names to see if I can pick up an accent, maybe they don't understand when I'm speaking to them.[22]

Why does Judge Pratt bother to take the extra time and effort to communicate in this way? She points to the fact that defendants "are making decisions, or having a judge make decisions about them, that will impact their relationships, their finances, and often their liberty," and that judges "have a responsibility to ensure that defendants make informed decisions." For Pratt, the stakes could not be higher: "The people who appear before me encounter violence daily. If I don't speak potential into somebody's life, the likelihood is that they don't come back to court—not because they've decided to sit at home and blow me off, but because they've been shot and killed."

The animating theory behind her judicial approach is simple: "I just get on the bench and treat people the way I would want my family members to be treated."

Judge Pratt is hardly alone in her efforts to communicate more effectively with defendants. Indeed, she credits Judge Alex Calabrese in New York with having influenced her practice. Judge Calabrese presides over the Red Hook Community Justice Center, a community-based courthouse in a geographically isolated neighborhood in southwest Brooklyn.

Like Newark Community Solutions, the Red Hook Community Justice Center was created by the Center for Court Innovation to expand the use of alternatives to incarceration for misdemeanor offenders. Each year the Justice Center links thousands of defendants to social services and community restitution projects in lieu of jail and fines.

Judge Alex Calabrese has presided over the Justice Center since the day it opened, and he is known throughout the community for his respectful approach. In the words of one defendant: "He allows you to speak. I got a good feel from Calabrese because of the fact that he likes to interact and get your opinion. I don't get the feeling that he's one of those judges that looks down on people. To me, he's fair, I'll put it that way."[23]

Judge Calabrese in Red Hook and Judge Pratt in Newark are living examples of an idea known as procedural justice. As advanced by Yale law professor Tom Tyler, the basic gist is that, while the outcome of your court case matters, so does the manner in which you were treated along the way. Everyone wants to win, of course, but Tyler suggests that people also want to be heard and to be respected. The implications of this insight are significant. In his seminal book *Why People Obey the Law*, Tyler makes the case that defendants who experience a justice process that they perceive to be fair and transparent are more likely to be law-abiding in the future. This is true regardless of whether or not they receive a favorable case outcome.

The experience of procedural justice is typically described as having several key elements, which include *voice* (were you given a chance to tell your side of the story?); *respect* (were you treated with dignity?); *neutrality* (did you perceive decision-makers as unbiased and trustworthy?); and *understanding* (did you understand your rights, obligations, and the decisions that were made about you?).[24]

Promoting procedural justice is important in individual

cases. The evidence suggests that by making defendants and victims feel better about their interactions with the justice system, it is possible to increase compliance with court orders. It is also important at a macro level because it has the potential to improve public perceptions of the legitimacy of laws and legal institutions.[25] Scholars like Tyler and his Yale colleague Tracey Meares have documented that in neighborhoods where there are high levels of mistrust, local residents are less likely to comply with the law.[26] In different ways (and using different language), thinkers as diverse as Robert Putnam, Robert Sampson, and Jane Jacobs have argued that trust is the glue that makes neighborhoods work.[27]

Wally Bazemore, a longtime community activist, sees the Red Hook Community Justice Center as an aid in bridging the gap that has long existed between police and local residents in particular: "They're not an occupying army. They work for us. As long as we stay within the realm of the law, they'll work with us."[28] Bazemore specifically credits Judge Calabrese for building trust in government: "We respect him as a judge, but he's part of our tribe, to put it succinctly. He's not an outsider. We don't look at him as an outsider. We look at him as an insider that's trying to make changes in our community for the better, for everybody, regardless of their color, social, economic standings or their . . . religious background or their gender—across the board."

MITIGATING A VICIOUS CYCLE

Of course, Newark and Red Hook aren't the only places where there is a need to bridge the gap between the justice system and the public it serves. In St. Louis, recent events have exposed a toxic relationship between communities of color and local government, much of it driven by the insight that the justice system was using fees and fines to balance budgets.[29]

Local reformers have recognized the need to reestablish trust between communities of color and the criminal justice system. "We want to focus on this idea of procedural justice," says Beth Huebner, a criminologist at the University of Missouri–St. Louis. "We want people to be able to trust the courts, to work with them."[30]

Procedural justice must be accompanied by changed practice. In addition to treating defendants with respect and dignity through their words, Judges Pratt and Calabrese do so through their deeds—working assiduously to avoid the unnecessary use of incarceration and fines. In Red Hook, independent researchers from the National Center for State Courts found profound cultural change. "Sentencing [at the Justice Center is] dramatically different from what prevails in the downtown courts," they wrote. "Fewer defendants receive jail sentences at Red Hook than in the comparison group. Compared to the downtown criminal court, the Justice Center increased the use of alternative community or social service sentences (78% at Red Hook versus 22% downtown) [and] decrease[d] the use of jail as a sentence (1% versus 15%)."[31]

Further, the researchers found "a robust and sustained decrease in the probability of recidivism in comparison to traditional misdemeanor case processing"—adult defendants were 10 percent less likely to be re-arrested, and juvenile defendants were 20 percent less likely.[32]

Our takeaway from all this is straightforward: marrying procedural justice to alternatives to jail and fines can reduce recidivism and increase public safety. The Justice Center has also improved the quality of life for many community residents, explains Alice Tapia, who grew up in Red Hook:

> I think a lot people have a certain way that they look at people who live in public housing. But not everybody is urinating in the elevators and drinking in public and stuff like that. That has to be addressed because the other half of the people that live there do not want to live like that. They want to live clean, and they want their places to be beautiful. . . . The biggest success of the court is actually holding the public accountable and responsible. Because of the court, a lot of people now think twice before they try to do something like take that leak in the elevator or before they break that bottle or before they commit one of those little petty crimes and stuff like that.[33]

These are the kinds of results that Mayor Ras Baraka is hoping to achieve in Newark. "When folks come in [to Newark

Community Solutions], we get to adjudicate them in nontra-ditional ways," he explains. "We've handed out over 9,000 hours of community service just this year alone." For Baraka, Newark Community Solutions amounts to an effort to "miti-gate a vicious cycle." The goal is to prevent the same defen-dants from shuffling through the system "over and over and over again."[34]

Nearly forty years ago, scholar Malcolm Feeley embed-ded himself in a court in New Haven, Connecticut, as part of the research for his landmark study *The Process Is the Pun-ishment: Handling Cases in a Lower Criminal Court.* A visit to the Newark Municipal Court today reveals many of the same conditions that Feeley chronicled back in 1979: crowded hall-ways, antiquated facilities, rapid-fire decision-making, and an atmosphere that more closely resembles a chaotic trading floor or a Middle Eastern shopping bazaar than a stately temple of justice.

Even in the face of these obstacles, Judge Pratt and her col-leagues are working to tame the Green Monster. By reducing the use of fines and short-term jail sentences while emphasiz-ing the values of kindness and common decency, the New-ark Municipal Court has made a significant commitment to change. Now the challenge is to sustain this effort over time—and to get other cities across the country to follow suit.

4

CALCULATED RISKS

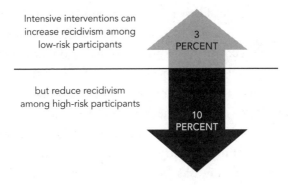

Intensive interventions can increase recidivism among low-risk participants

3 PERCENT

but reduce recidivism among high-risk participants

10 PERCENT

High-risk and low-risk offenders need to be treated differently[1]

Addressing a crowded room at the National Press Club in Washington, D.C., in October 2011, John Jay College President Jeremy Travis framed the project of criminal justice reform in these terms: "If we want our response to crime to be more effective and more humane . . . we must summon the assistance of two powerful superheroes—two forces that, working together, can sweep away the cobwebs in our minds, clear the highest organizational hurdles and move political mountains. Our two superheroes are science—the quest for empirical truth—and passion—the human impulse to seek justice."[2]

In the years since Travis's speech, a growing number of criminal justice reformers have embraced his call for a greater emphasis on science. These reformers have argued that strategies rooted in rigorous scientific research and statistical analysis are the long-sought corrective to our overreliance on incarceration.

Tim Murray is one of these reformers. Murray has spent the bulk of his career trying to reform government from the inside, but in recent years he has moved outside of government, devoting his energies to the Pretrial Justice Institute. "How did we get to be a nation that has so many of our people behind bars?" Murray asks. "How did we get to be the world's leader in this awful practice of putting people in cages? How did we get to this state of play in the face of science that shows us time after time after time we're making things worse, not better? Well, it's because it's the way we've always done it."[3]

Advocates like Murray point to the use of money bail as a major contributor to expanding incarceration. The stated purpose of bail is to ensure a defendant's appearance at trial following an arrest. The idea is simple: if you know you will lose a few thousand bucks, you are more likely to show up in court when you are supposed to.

For many defendants, bail works just fine. But what about those who don't have a few thousand dollars to spare—or even a few hundred? These people end up in jail, waiting behind bars for their cases to reach a conclusion.

There are a number of problems with this situation. First is a basic question of justice. Remember: these individuals have not been found guilty of any offense. In our system of jurisprudence, they are presumed innocent. Indeed, some will ultimately win their cases. Why should they spend any time at all in jail?

Then there is the problem of coercion. Spending time in jail is so unpleasant that many defendants will do anything they can to avoid it—including agreeing to unfavorable plea bargains that saddle them with criminal convictions and other onerous conditions. Jail time essentially tips the delicate balance of the criminal justice system away from defendants and toward prosecutors.

Finally, there is the problem of long-term impact. Holding thousands of defendants in jail while their cases are pending probably does yield some public safety benefits—after all, you can't commit crimes while you are detained. But these short-term incapacitation benefits must be weighed against the lasting effects of spending time in jail. Researchers are increasingly coming to the conclusion that even short stays in jail can increase criminal behavior, turning minor miscreants into hardened criminals.[4]

THE SCIENCE OF ASSESSMENT

Not long after Travis's speech, Anne Milgram, of the Laura and John Arnold Foundation, wrote an article for *The Atlantic* entitled "Moneyballing Criminal Justice."[5] Describing the use of data analytics to transform such disparate industries as professional baseball and health care, Milgram argued for using similar statistical methods to improve the field of criminal justice:

> Technology could help us leverage data to identify offenders who will pose unacceptable risks to society if they are not behind bars and distinguish them from those defendants who will have lower recidivism rates if they are supervised in the community or given alternatives to incarceration before trial. Likewise, it could help us figure out which terms of imprisonment, alternatives to incarceration, and other interventions work best—and for whom.

As Milgram makes clear, criminal justice has come a long way since the 1970s. Back then, sociologist Robert Martinson became famous for trumpeting the idea that "nothing works" to rehabilitate individuals involved in the criminal justice system.[6] Martinson's work, which was later debunked, had an enormous impact. Indeed, it was one of the hidden causes of mass incarceration, lending academic credence to tough-on-crime criminal justice policies that heavily favored the use of incarceration over community-based alternatives.

In the years since Martinson, researchers have documented that there are safe and effective alternatives to incarceration, such as drug treatment, vocational education, and targeted therapies.[7] If executed properly and under the right set of circumstances, these kinds of community-based interventions can make a difference for many (but not all) individuals.

This raises a critical question: How can we determine who is an appropriate candidate for a community-based intervention instead of jail or prison? The Risk–Need–Responsivity model offers an answer. Initially developed in the 1980s, the model is supported by nearly four hundred separate studies.[8] "When Don Andrews and Jim Bonta developed the model, it was in response to people who had just gone around saying that nothing works," recalls Kelly Hannah-Moffat, a criminologist at the University of Toronto. "They said, 'Well, wait a minute. That's not so true. We need to figure out what works.' "[9]

At the heart of the Risk–Need–Responsivity model is the idea that it is possible to make more informed decisions about who is potentially dangerous and who isn't. Using statistical information from hundreds of thousands of previous cases, researchers can create assessment instruments capable of measuring the risk of re-offending posed by individual defendants. Dozens of such instruments are currently being used across the country. Most look closely at an individual's criminal record and history of appearing in court. Some take into account other factors, such as whether an individual has a job, a stable housing situation, or a problem with drugs or alcohol. No two instruments are exactly alike, and accuracy can vary widely.

But all of the tools seek to group individuals into different categories, determining who is at high risk of re-offense, who is at low risk, and who is in between.

The second big idea embedded in the Risk-Need-Responsivity model is that any intervention offered by the justice system should be directly tied to participants' level of risk. The crucial and perhaps counterintuitive point here is this: intensive interventions like long-term residential drug treatment are most effective with higher-risk individuals and can actually be counterproductive with lower-risk individuals.[10]

Why is this? In general, low-risk individuals tend to have some positive attributes in their lives—they have jobs, they have families, they go to church, they are enrolled in school. Intensive interventions like residential drug treatment tend to take participants away from these things. Just as important, they tend to introduce low-risk individuals to a new peer group: high-risk individuals. This can create a contagion effect, turning low-risk people into high-risk people—the school-of-crime theory. "There is a clear harm that's done when we focus on low-risk people," explains University of Cincinnati criminologist Edward Latessa. "We're disrupting them. We're making them worse."[11]

The upshot is that judges and other criminal justice actors should look to off-ramp lower-risk individuals as soon as possible with little or no formal intervention. Of course, this runs contrary to the instincts of many policymakers, who tend to be more comfortable talking about community programs instead of jail for low-risk defendants. But the Risk-Need-Responsivity model suggests that the opposite is true: the best candidates for long-term drug treatment and residential programs are moderate- and high-risk defendants. In general, lower-risk individuals should be sentenced to the least disruptive sanctions available: community service or a few sessions meeting with a counselor or, in many cases, nothing at all. High-risk defendants, by contrast, are more likely to benefit from being removed from their surroundings to a rehabilitative setting.

So there is a disconnect between what the science says and the gut instincts of those who run the criminal justice system. Traditionally, when this happens, gut instincts win. This is particularly true when defendants have engaged in violent behavior. In these cases, the public is less likely to accept a community-based sentence, even if the data show that mandated treatment is more likely to be effective than incarceration. According to Edward Latessa, "The public's less tolerant of violent acts. They want violent people held accountable. So that's the . . . demarcation line."

Jennifer Skeem, a clinical psychologist and professor at the University of California at Berkeley, thinks drawing the line at violence is ill-advised:

> I come from a background where I've focused a lot on high-risk juveniles and high-risk adults. It's really clear that, if they're provided with sufficient doses of

treatment, you see pretty impressive violence-reduction effects. I think that, if part of the interest here is not just reducing mass incarceration or saving money, and part of the interest is in actually making a difference when it comes to public safety, then it is a mistake to cut out "violent offenders" or serious offenders from [treatment programs].[12]

In general, a low-risk or a high-risk designation on an assessment tool isn't a foolproof predictor of behavior—it is simply an estimate based on how other people with similar characteristics have performed in the past. As they say in the investment industry, past performance is no guarantee of future results. This cuts in both directions. Sometimes low-risk people end up committing heinous crimes. And sometimes high-risk people can beat the odds. Bradley Jacobs, who helped to oversee behavioral health programs at the Center for Alternative Sentencing and Employment Services (CASES), an alternative-to-incarceration program in New York City, offers an example of one such defendant:

He was in and out of the hospital, substance use, living on the streets, didn't really engage in treatment early on . . . scored off the charts [on a risk assessment tool]. It was basically, I think, a 99 percent chance that it was likely he'd get rearrested. I think it was a violent felony he came in on. If you had done all that work before admitting him, you would screen him out. You'd say, "There's no way you're going to be effective. What's the point?" . . . He actually succeeded. He made it through the program.[13]

Cornell University law professor Joseph Margulies observes that elected officials often portray "a Manichaean world that divides the prison population between the harmless few and the predatory many."[14] Real life is not that simple.

Risk assessment is not an exact science. But, in the aggregate, it is massively superior to what constitutes business as usual at the moment: judges and prosecutors and other criminal justice officials making decisions about who should be in jail and who shouldn't with little information beyond a rap sheet and their own instincts and inherent biases.

EVIDENCE-BASED PROGRAMS

According to the Risk-Need-Responsivity model, rehabilitative interventions are most effective when they are calibrated to address the particular strengths and challenges of individual participants. Cognitive-behavioral therapy is one such intervention.

"Thinking controls behavior," explains Juliana Taymans, George Washington University professor and one of the creators of Thinking for a Change, a widely used cognitive-behavioral program. "The key to behavior change is to know how our thoughts, feelings, attitudes, and beliefs guide our actions."[15] Researchers have shown that, by encouraging self-awareness, cognitive-behavioral therapy can improve mood regulation, impulse control, and anger management among participants. Interventions like cognitive-behavioral therapy that have been subject to rigorous study by researchers and documented to have an impact have become known in the field by a simple shorthand: "evidence-based programs." (For more on cognitive-behavioral therapy and Thinking for a Change, see chapter 6.)

In recent years, the U.S. Department of Justice has made a significant investment in spreading the use of such programs. This development should be celebrated. In many respects, we are living through a golden age when it comes to criminal justice research. We know more than we ever have before about the kinds of programs that actually make a difference. And policymakers at all levels of government have grown more sophisticated about what the research says about specific interventions.

But we should beware of overselling. The language of "evidence-based programs" and "what works" clearinghouses suggests that we have easy answers for how to reduce the use of incarceration. This is not the case.

Take cognitive-behavioral therapy. Researchers have documented that if an individual has a 40 percent likelihood of re-offending, cognitive-behavioral programs can lower this likelihood, on average, to 30 percent. (Cognitive-behavioral therapy has been shown to achieve greater reductions with higher-risk individuals.) [16]

While this is good news, it may come as a disappointment to some. No intervention guarantees success for every offender who participates in it. Even an evidence-based intervention like cognitive-behavioral therapy fails to change the behavior of many participants.

There are no easy, off-the-shelf solutions when it comes to changing the behavior of offending populations. Many parts of the country also do not have access to evidence-based programs. And even where these programs do exist, there is no guarantee that they have been implemented with care, skill, or fidelity to the underlying model.

The success of cognitive-behavioral therapy depends largely on the skills of the person charged with facilitating the groups. Workbooks and protocols and training sessions will get you part of the way there, but in the end, there is no substitute for a thoughtful facilitator with the flexibility to adapt as the situation requires. [17]

It also takes a considerable amount of time or "dosage" for cognitive-behavioral treatment to reduce recidivism. One study found that upwards of three hundred hours were necessary to significantly reduce recidivism among higher-risk individuals with complicated needs. [18] This poses serious logistical challenges. It is difficult to keep participants engaged over the course of dozens of sessions. In general, the longer the intervention, the more likely it will be difficult for an individual to complete—and the harder it will be for a program to be well implemented.

Things fall apart. Edward Latessa, of the University of Cincinnati, who has dedicated the bulk of his professional life to spreading evidence-based programs, has experienced this reality firsthand:

> Here's what frustrates us. We'll go into a jurisdiction. They'll spend a lot of money. We'll train them, and we'll coach them, and then six months later, it all falls apart. It falls apart because of lack of leadership. It falls apart because they don't build capacity well. They don't understand how to sustain it. That's very frustrating. I've worked all over the country. We've redesigned, for example, a number of juvenile residential programs in Ohio. Now we do quarterly visits, and we do monitoring of them. Many of them are falling back into the same old bad habits that they had before.[19]

As Latessa makes plain, implementation challenges in criminal justice are real and formidable. Significant energy has gone into overcoming these challenges in recent years. A veritable cottage industry of trainers and consultants has emerged to explain the Risk-Need-Responsivity model. All of these efforts are predicated on the notion that the primary obstacles to advancing evidence-based reforms are ignorance and cultural resistance to change. After all, who could be against something as commonsensical as basing criminal justice decisions on what the social science research says?

THE RISK OF BIAS

And then Attorney General Eric Holder entered the fray. "Holder Cautions on Risk of Bias in Big Data Use in Criminal Justice," reported the *Wall Street Journal*.[20] "How We Imprison the Poor for Crimes That Haven't Happened Yet," read *Gawker*.[21] "One Popular Fix for Mass Incarceration Could Make Racial Disparities Even Worse," cautioned *Vox*.[22]

What was going on here?

Speaking to the National Association of Criminal Defense Lawyers in the summer of 2014, Holder expressed grave concerns about the idea that judges would use risk assessments to inform their decisions. Holder warned of judges using "the possibility of a future crime that has not taken place" to make determinations about jail and prison in the here and now. He cautioned, "we need to be sure the use of aggregate data analysis won't have unintended consequences."[23]

Holder's concerns were based on a basic truth: assessment instruments typically predict risk based on criminal history information. The algorithms vary from instrument to instrument, but almost all of them take into account such factors as prior arrests, failure to appear in court on prior cases, and the existence of unresolved cases.[24]

In general, risk assessment instruments place tremendous

weight on variables that are both immutable and highly related to socioeconomic disadvantage. A defendant can't change her rap sheet, past performance in school, or employment history no matter how hard she tries. Social science tells us that these factors are highly predictive of future criminal behavior; experience tells us that these kinds of factors are also heavily influenced by a defendant's race, class, gender, and sexual identity. Critics like Holder have argued that risk assessment is built on a shaky foundation. If bias exists in the criminal justice system with regard to how certain groups are policed and prosecuted and adjudicated, creating assessment tools that rely on past criminal history may simply compound that bias.

Another problem is the reality that assessment tools are based on the aggregate behavior of large groups of offenders. They tell decision-makers about how other people who share the same characteristics as the defendant before them today have behaved in the past.

What the tools have to say about any individual defendant is open to debate.[25] "Human behavior is not predictable," says criminologist Faye S. Taxman. "It's the fundamental problem."[26] No risk assessment tool on the market can measure motivation to change. "What risk assessment tools can't measure is the power of redemption, a human capacity that belongs to people who have committed all sorts of crimes," writes Glenn E. Martin, the founder of JustLeadershipUSA.[27]

On the heels of Holder's speech, the *New York Times* ran an op-ed by University of Michigan law professor Sonja B. Starr, claiming that the trend toward risk assessment amounted to racial profiling and would further exacerbate the problems of mass incarceration. Starr did not mince words:

> The United States inarguably has a mass-incarceration crisis, but it is poor people and minorities who bear its brunt. Punishment profiling will exacerbate these disparities—including racial disparities—because the risk assessments include many race-correlated variables. Profiling sends the toxic message that the state considers certain groups of people dangerous based on their identity. It also confirms the widespread impression that the criminal justice system is rigged against the poor.[28]

Columbia law professor Bernard E. Harcourt summarized the argument: "the fact is, risk today has collapsed into prior criminal history, and prior criminal history has become a proxy for race."[29]

Ironically, many evidence-based reformers view risk assessment as a tool to *mitigate* the effects of bias and other vagaries of human subjectivity. "The 'compared to what' for risk assessment is judges' intuitive impressions about risk," says Jennifer Skeem, of the University of California at Berkeley. "They're human, and their human judgments are, we know from related research, pretty prone to error compared to these risk assessment tools."

"Decisions to detain are often highly subjective and

personal," explains Mark Soler, executive director of the Center for Children's Law and Policy.[30] "They're influenced by the appearance of the child and the family, and sometimes what neighborhood they live in."

In 2015, the Brennan Center for Justice hosted a roundtable to discuss the reduction of racial and ethnic disparities in American jails. Participants, including Georgetown University law professor Paul Butler, Glenn Martin of JustLeadership USA, and Marc Mauer of the Sentencing Project, made it clear that the use of prior criminal history to predict a defendant's level of risk reflects racial and socioeconomic disparities in policing and arrest practices. Nonetheless, there was also a strong sense that an imperfect science is still preferable to no science at all.[31]

Even Sonja Starr acknowledges that, absent persuasive evidence, it is "hard to fight peoples' intuition that when somebody strikes us as scary, we should lock them up."[32] Starr is essentially making the case for risk assessment. Experience suggests that these tools can provide the kind of evidence that many decision-makers find persuasive.

Just as important, risk assessment tools also provide a measure of political cover. If judges and prosecutors are making decisions about who to release and who to detain based on their gut instincts alone, there is no one else to blame when things go wrong. This breeds conservatism—no judge or prosecutor wants to find themselves held responsible when a defendant they have released commits a new crime. But the picture changes, at least somewhat, when a risk assessment instrument is introduced into the mix. Then, judges and prosecutors can point to an objective risk assessment score to validate their decision. This can provide a measure of political safety and breed more thoughtful decision-making.

SPOCK AND BONES

From our perspective, the operative question is how to maximize the benefits of risk assessments while safeguarding against their limitations.

In general, modesty should be our watchword. The field should proceed on the view that there is still more to learn and a lot of room for improvement. This means encouraging greater transparency among those who create risk assessment tools about how the tools weigh different factors and about how accurate their instruments are. This means engaging on-the-ground practitioners in developing and refining risk assessment tools rather than forcing them to use prepackaged protocols that undermine or constrain their professional discretion. And this means looking at how risk assessment tools impact racial outcomes in the justice system—and making adjustments as necessary.

There is an undeniable tension between an aggregate analysis of the justice system ("we incarcerate too many people of color") and the realities of life in the courts, where defendants must be handled one by one and each case reflects unique circumstances and contexts. Judges and attorneys and probation officers have tough jobs. When a case goes bad, it is their reputation on the line—and their names in the newspaper.

In addition to modesty, the use of risk assessment tools and evidence-based programs should be guided by a fundamental belief in human dignity. Glenn Martin of JustLeadershipUSA warns of the dangers of advancing "an automated and mechanical solution to a bizarre and inhumane system."[33] Martin is of course talking primarily about defendants, but the same holds true for the people who staff our justice system, many of whom feel they work in dreadful environments and bear the burden of unrealistic expectations.

As Jeremy Travis made clear at the National Press Club in 2011, science alone cannot solve the problems of our justice system—it must be tempered with compassion.[34] We need to channel both Mr. Spock and Dr. Leonard "Bones" McCoy from *Star Trek* if we are to reduce the use of incarceration. We need a Spock-ian commitment to rational decision-making that moves away from bias and emotion to make more reasoned judgments about defendants. But, like Bones, we also need to recognize the fundamental humanity—and capacity for change—of every person in the justice system, no matter what side of the law they happen to be on. Only by marrying these approaches can we hope to have a justice system that is both effective and humane.

5

RISK, RELEASE, AND RIKERS ISLAND

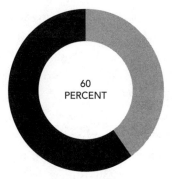

Over **60 percent** of the U.S. jail population consists of individuals awaiting trial[1]

Two thousand sixteen was a year of intense focus on criminal justice reform in New York City—demonstrations on the steps of City Hall, impassioned editorials in the papers, lawsuits filed, and new initiatives launched. But perhaps no single event reverberated longer or louder than the State of the City speech that was delivered by New York City Council Speaker Melissa Mark-Viverito in the spring of that year.

In her address, Mark-Viverito announced the creation of an independent commission, to be chaired by former New York State chief judge Jonathan Lippman, that would be charged with creating a new blueprint for justice in New York City. The goal? To find ways to get the city's jail population on Rikers Island "to be so small that the dream of shutting it down becomes a reality."[2]

With that single line, Mark-Viverito added fuel to a conversation that was already gathering momentum in the offices of local advocacy groups and foundations. Was it possible to close one of the largest and most notorious jail complexes in the United States?

Twenty-five years ago, the answer would have been obvious: no way. There were simply too many people on Rikers Island to imagine closing the facility. In the early 1990s, the average daily head count on Rikers Island was more than 20,000 people. Today, the daily population is typically less than 10,000.[3]

New York's success in reducing its jail population over the past generation is worth celebrating both on its own terms and because it goes against the grain of a national trend: between 1980 and 2008, the number of inmates housed in a local jail on any given day in the United States increased by 426 percent (from 184,000 to 785,500).[4]

It may hold fewer people than it used to, but Rikers Island is still a powerful symbol of the harms wrought by the overuse of incarceration. The problems on Rikers Island aren't a secret. Indeed, they are national news. In 2014, a U.S. Department of Justice investigation found "a pattern and practice of conduct that violated the rights of adolescents."[5] U.S. Attorney Preet

Bharara, a fierce critic, identified a "deep-seated culture of violence" on the island.[6]

In 2015, Jennifer Gonnerman, writing in *The New Yorker*, told the tragic story of Kalief Browder.[7] Accused of stealing a backpack at sixteen, Browder spent three years in pretrial detention on Rikers Island, including a lengthy stay in solitary confinement. Security footage confirmed Browder's accounts of repeated beatings at the hands of both correction officers and fellow inmates.

Despite being offered plea deals that would have resulted in his immediate release, Browder maintained his innocence, and the charges against him were eventually dropped.[8] Although he was ultimately released, Browder struggled to find his footing in the community. He committed suicide just a few months after becoming a local cause célèbre. Browder's experience on Rikers Island has become a powerful rallying cry for opponents of solitary confinement and advocates of jail reduction.

At this point, few serious analysts dispute the fact that Rikers can do real harm to inmates, undermining their mental health and sabotaging their educational and employment prospects. But that's not where the problems end. Rikers is also one of the most expensive jails in America. In 2015, New York City spent almost $2.4 billion on incarceration: $1.1 billion for the Department of Correction and $1.3 billion for other agencies performing work related to Rikers and the city's other jail facilities.[9]

These costs, dear as they are, might easily be borne if it could be demonstrated that Rikers were essential to the safety of New York City. But the numbers do not support this argument. To be sure, there is some incapacitation benefit to detaining people; while they are confined on Rikers Island, inmates cannot do harm to the general public. But that benefit is exceedingly limited. Many inmates spend only a few days or weeks on Rikers Island. The short-term benefits of jail must be weighed against the long-term impacts. Over the long haul, sending someone to Rikers Island can actually undermine public safety by disconnecting inmates from positive influences and creating more hardened criminals. "Even if its inmates were not brutalized, its guards not thuggish, its corridors not afflicted by gangs, weapons and drugs," writes the *New York Times* editorial board, "Rikers would still be a bad idea." [10]

A NOBLE CONCEPT

If Rikers Island is a bad idea, why not simply get rid of it? This was City Council Speaker Melissa Mark-Viverito's logic as she prepared her State of the City address. But New York City politics being what they are, her dream of shuttering the jail received a mixed response.

New York State governor Andrew M. Cuomo immediately embraced closing Rikers as a "big solution" to a "big problem." [11] New York City mayor Bill de Blasio was less enthusiastic. While acknowledging the "noble concept," de Blasio

86

cited an array of pragmatic challenges. "The problem is, it would cost many billions of dollars," explained de Blasio. "I have to look out for what's feasible and I have to look out for the taxpayer."[12] New York City Police Commissioner William J. Bratton hit a similar note: "It sounds nice. Let's close Rikers Island. Do you want to put a jail beside your house in Staten Island or in Queens or in Manhattan? We're already having a problem with homeless shelters that people are concerned with. So who wants to house 10,000 prisoners in their neighborhood?"[13] Bratton's concerns proved well founded. Before Mark-Viverito's independent commission had even begun its work, local politicians lined up to be the first to proclaim: not in my backyard.

"Any correctional facility in my district or on Staten Island is a non-starter for me," declared New York City Council Member Steven Matteo. Council Member Joseph Borelli echoed the sentiment: "Nobody wants to have a revolving door of perpetrators in their community." Council Member Paul Vallone promised a "fierce and complete opposition" in response to any attempts to site a new jail in his district in Queens.[14]

Despite these ominous noises, Mark-Viverito's commission ended up recommending that the City of New York shutter Rikers Island and move to a smaller, state-of-the-art jail system that would include facilities located near the criminal courthouses in each of New York's five boroughs.[15] The commission's chair, Jonathan Lippman, said, "Rikers Island is not just physically remote—it is psychologically isolated from the rest of New York City. Rikers severs connections with families and communities, with harmful consequences for anyone who spends even a few days on the Island. . . . Put simply, it is a 19th-century solution to a 21st century problem." [16]

Lippman was hardly alone in reaching this conclusion. Three of the five elected district attorneys in New York signed on to the idea of closing Rikers. They were joined by hundreds of grassroots activists organized by the #Closerikers campaign led by JustLeadershipUSA and the Katal Center for Health, Equity, and Justice.

And then, dramatically, they were joined by New York City Mayor Bill de Blasio. In March 2017, Mayor de Blasio announced his intention to close the troubled jail complex on Rikers Island. "This is a very serious, sober, forever decision," de Blasio said. [17]

In making this decision, de Blasio emphasized that before Rikers can be closed, the city must first figure out how to reduce the jail population still further. The city is currently pursuing a range of strategies to accomplish this goal.

One answer is to bring fewer people into the system. For example, local police and prosecutors have made the decision to essentially decriminalize the possession of small amounts of marijuana. The city council has picked up on this theme, encouraging the police to use civil, rather than criminal, penalties for a range of minor misbehavior.

For those cases that do make it to court, the city is work-ing to streamline the bail payment process, thereby increasing the number of defendants who can make bail and be released instead of being transported to Rikers Island. The city is also collaborating with the court system in an effort to expedite case processing, moving cases to conclusion as quickly as possible.

But perhaps the best hope for reducing New York City's jail population is a new, citywide pretrial supervised release pro-gram. The vast majority of inmates on Rikers Island (approxi-mately 75 percent) are pretrial detainees, meaning defendants with pending criminal cases.[18] Some of these pretrial detainees have been arrested for heinous offenses—rape, murder, arson. And some are charged with minor crimes—drug possession, shoplifting, trespass, and the like. Those who find themselves on Rikers Island have been assigned bail amounts that they cannot afford to meet. Often these bail amounts are surpris-ingly small—$2,000 or less.[19] This has led many to conclude that poverty is the driving factor determining who is jailed and who is not.[20]

In theory, pretrial detention should be used in cases when a defendant is a threat to public safety. But research suggests that each year, New York City locks up thousands of people who present a limited risk of re-offense.[21] Where's the sense in that?

This is a question that has begun to trouble many front-line practitioners. One of them is Judge George Grasso, who presides over a busy arraignment court in the Bronx. Many of the defendants he sees hardly qualify as criminal masterminds. He describes a typical case:

> If you have somebody, for example, that is getting arrested for criminal possession of a controlled substance in the seventh degree, because they're in some alley at two o'clock in the morning snorting crack cocaine, typically the way we handle a person like that, over and over and over, is we put bail on them. They don't make bail. They go to Rikers Island. We just look at the rap sheet. We say, "Well, you know you've done this seven or eight times so now it's going to be thirty days' jail, forty-five days' jail. Go to Rikers." They come out of Rikers. They do the same thing and we do the same thing. Not only do I think we are not serving the needs of the individual, I don't think we're serving the needs of public safety.[22]

MODELS OF CHANGE

"The current pretrial system is broken and the fix is pretty easy," says Cherise Fanno Burdeen of the Pretrial Justice Institute. "In the world of hard things, this isn't one of them."[23] Advocates like Burdeen point to research that shows that forty-eight hours or more in jail is enough to do real damage to defendants, increasing their likelihood of becoming chronic offenders.[24] "Lower-risk defendants come out worse than when they went in," explains Burdeen. "Anything that was helping them be lower-risk is disrupted after even a few days in jail—jobs, housing, family connections."

Accordingly, pretrial reformers are working to encourage cities like New York to release more defendants, with or without formal supervision, during the pretrial period. In doing so, they are pushing the justice system to live up to Chief Justice William Rehnquist's declaration that "[i]n our society, liberty is the norm, and detention prior to trial or without trial is the carefully limited exception."[25] The American Bar Association has defined this carefully limited exception as a circumstance in which "no condition or combination of conditions of release will reasonably ensure the defendant's appearance in court or protect the safety of the community."[26] The idea here is that along with the bedrock presumption of innocence in the United States comes a second, related presumption: pretrial freedom from confinement.

Despite this aspiration, the reality is that over 60 percent of the U.S. jail population consists of individuals awaiting trial—the accused, not the convicted.[27] According to Tim Murray, of the Pretrial Justice Institute, "The vast majority of these individuals could, in fact, be released had they access to the financial resources that have been required by the court. We know money doesn't do anything to ameliorate risk. It simply keeps people in jail who don't have it."[28]

One place this isn't happening is Washington, D.C. "The DC jail is below 50 percent of its capacity, with virtually no one there because of their inability to post a monetary bond as a condition of release," notes Clifford T. Keenan, who heads up the Pretrial Services Agency for the District of Columbia.[29] According to Keenan, nine out of ten defendants in Washington are released (either on their own recognizance or with supervision) while their cases are pending. Each defendant in Washington is assessed to determine whether they are a risk to commit further offenses. According to Keenan, based on this information:

> We work with the judges to fashion the least restrictive conditions necessary to assure community safety and return to court. Research in the pretrial field has shown that imposing too many conditions on low- and moderate-risk defendants will likely have negative consequences. For low-risk individuals, we recommend release on personal recognizance with no other conditions; for the very high-risk, we say that there are no conditions that we can recommend to assure return to court or community safety. For those in between, we recommend a variety of conditions depending upon the individual circumstances.

Release conditions for individuals in the latter category might include a curfew, electronic monitoring, in-person reporting, and drug testing.

On a typical day in Washington, D.C., about seventy-four

individuals will end up being charged with a new crime.[30] Of these seventy-four, sixty-six will remain in the community while their case is processed (eight will be held on the order of a judge). Two of the sixty-six will be immediately placed into a high-intensity supervision program, which requires weekly in-person reporting, GPS tracking, drug testing, and other conditions. The rest will be released on personal recognizance (no conditions at all) or to a less-intensive supervision regimen.[31]

According to Keenan, the overwhelming majority of defendants who are released in Washington, D.C., show up on their court dates and avoid re-arrest: "Of those who are released, we find that 88 percent make all of their scheduled court appearances and about 89 percent remain arrest-free during their pretrial status. Of those who are re-arrested, it is mainly for a low level offense, as we find less than 2 percent of those released are re-arrested for a violent crime."[32]

Many of the ingredients from Washington, D.C., are also being tested in Kentucky—with similar results. According to Tara Blair, who oversees Kentucky's statewide pretrial services program, "We use a risk assessment and avoid supervising lower-risk defendants. . . . High-risk defendants are recommended for release with supervision to mitigate the risk."[33] Blair proudly cites "a release rate of 73 percent and an appearance rate of 88 percent, with 90 percent of defendants not being charged with new crimes while their cases are pending."

What does supervised release look like in practice? To

Mark Heyerly, of the Kentucky Court of Justice's Division of Pretrial Services, a twenty-three-year-old man named Peter was a typical client.

Peter was riding a motorcycle when he was stopped by police. The police officer discovered that the motorcycle had been reported stolen a few days prior. Although he told the officer that the motorcycle belonged to a friend and he was only borrowing it, Peter was arrested for receiving stolen property, a Class D felony.

Using an assessment tool, a pretrial officer determined that Peter was low risk, meaning that he was unlikely to re-offend. The risk score was based on Peter's current charge and his criminal history, which included a few prior convictions for misdemeanors, but no felony convictions and no prior failures to appear in court. Based at least in part on the low-risk designation, the judge in the case released Peter on the condition that he have no further contact with the motorcycle.

The case took approximately a month to resolve. Peter showed up for his court dates and ultimately pled guilty to a misdemeanor charge of attempting to receive stolen property. He did not receive a jail sentence. The final tally: nearly four weeks of pretrial detention avoided, no new crimes committed.[34] Everyone won in this scenario. Peter got a chance to stay at home and keep his life together. And the government did not have to devote precious resources to jailing him needlessly.

Not every case is so simple, of course. Some arrestees pose a greater risk to public safety or come to court with greater needs, including addiction, joblessness, and mental illness. Heyerly offers a more complicated example from his files: the case of Reed.

Thirty-two years old, Reed was arrested on felony-level drug possession charges involving methamphetamine, heroin, a crack pipe, and a hypodermic needle. He had a lengthy criminal history, which included past drug-related convictions, as well as failing to appear for court on multiple occasions. As a result, Reed was assessed to be high risk.

The judge in the case ultimately decided to take a chance on Reed. He was released with the requirement that he meet with a pretrial officer every week. He also had to submit to random drug testing and avoid any criminal behavior.

Reed's first drug test came back positive for marijuana. Fortunately for Reed, judges and prosecutors in Kentucky are well aware that marijuana can appear on drug screens for up to thirty days after use—and this first test occurred less than two weeks after his arrest. Reed remained in the community, and all of his subsequent drug tests were negative. Three months later, Reed showed up for his court date and pled guilty to a lesser charge of attempted drug possession. All other pending charges were dismissed, and he did not receive a jail sentence. That's the good news. The bad news is that unless Reed's substance abuse is treated, his risk of recidivism will remain high. The hope in Kentucky and other places with vibrant supervised release programs is that a few weeks of pretrial services, be it short-term help with education, training, treatment, or counseling, will spur defendants to seek out long-term services on a voluntary basis.

Peter and Reed were very different defendants. One was just starting out in life, with a minor record of criminal involvement. The other had been in and out of jail for quite some time. What these examples demonstrate is that there are pretrial solutions for both low- and high-risk defendants that avoid the use of incarceration without jeopardizing public safety.

So why isn't every place like Kentucky or Washington? Opposition can come from a variety of quarters.

Herbert Bernsen, who oversees the local jail in St. Louis County, has worked to bring pretrial reform to St. Louis. While many local players acknowledged that jail overcrowding was a problem, Bernsen found that "[j]udges were often reluctant to approve pretrial release without prior approval from the prosecutor's office."[35]

David K. Byers, administrative director of the courts in Arizona, gets to the heart of judges' reluctance to embrace pretrial release:

> If you talk to judges honestly, they are always worried about picking up the paper one morning and seeing somebody they released committing a heinous crime. It goes through their mind every day when they're making decisions to release people. I think, historically, there's been some comfort for judges imposing some

sort of bail. Now if they bail out and still commit a crime, at least there was a bail imposed, the judge just didn't release them.[36]

Prosecutors worry too. "District attorneys want to get re-elected," says George Gascón, San Francisco's district attorney. "And a lot of the elected district attorneys around this country today were elected, and have been reelected, on tough-on-crime platforms." At the end of the day, says Gascón, "a lot of what they do is motivated by the fear factor of staying employed."[37]

BACK TO NEW YORK

The obstacles to change are particularly significant in New York City. Glenn Martin, a former inmate on Rikers Island who runs the advocacy group JustLeadershipUSA, paints a bleak portrait of the prospects for real change in New York City:

First, the bail industry would be the biggest opponent. . . . Second, the problem with suggesting that pretrial diversion is the way to go is that no one has an appetite for this—even our mayor. Everyone is concerned about the one case that is not going to go well. I hate to tell people, but that is the nature of criminal justice. If we continue to make policy based on that one case that might not go well, we are going to stay stuck right where we are. That is what got us here. What got us here is a bunch of criminal justice policy-making that made for good politics and bad policy, and all of it was based on that one horrendous case. Think of how many laws we have that are named after young white children that unfortunately were killed or hurt or maimed at the hands of someone who should not have been [there] or should have been in [prison]. We have heard the stories over and over—the Willie Horton stories.[38]

Despite Martin's dire analysis, change is happening in New York City. By creating supervised release programs in each borough, the city is attempting to reduce the flow of defendants from criminal court to Rikers Island. "It is a common sense approach that balances public safety and liberty by expanding the options available to judges beyond simply detention or release with no conditions," says Elizabeth Glazer, director of the Mayor's Office of Criminal Justice.[39]

How do these goals get translated into action on the ground? A visit to 120 Schermerhorn Street, the centralized criminal court in Brooklyn, offers some clues.

The first thing you learn watching arraignments in Brooklyn Criminal Court is that a large percentage of cases are resolved at the first court appearance—something like four out of ten cases.[40] The second thing you learn is that even those cases that are continued for one reason or another—because the defendant doesn't want to plead guilty or the prosecutor wants to go to trial or some other factor—often do not result in pretrial detention. In New York City, the vast majority (71 percent) of defendants whose cases continue are released on their own recognizance.[41] They must return to court for their subsequent court dates, but they are under no formal supervision. (By way of comparison, a national study of pretrial release trends from 1990 to 2004 found only 32 percent released on their own recognizance.[42])

Despite all of this, because of New York City's size, and the sheer volume of criminal court activity, bail is still being set in thousands of cases. And this means that thousands of individuals are still being detained on Rikers Island.

Adam, a forty-year-old father of four, might have been one of them. He was arrested and charged with stealing a bicycle. His lawyer was concerned about the prospect of bail being set, so she requested a screening to determine his eligibility for supervised release. This was performed by a case manager at Brooklyn Justice Initiatives, the supervised release program for the county.[43]

When Adam's case was called, the prosecutor requested $2,500 bail—a price that he and his family could not afford to pay. Many defendants turn to the bail bonds industry when they are faced with this situation. These are private businesses that provide cash as a guarantee that a defendant will appear in court. The defendant is charged a fee in return for this service, typically a percentage of the bail amount. The problem for defendants like Adam is that the bail amounts that they face (and the resulting fees they generate) are so small that it is not worth the effort for bail bondsmen to post bail on their behalf. These defendants are caught between a rock and a hard place—they don't have the money they need, but they can't turn to bail bondsmen for help because there is literally no profit in it.

Knowing all of this, Adam's defense attorney requested that he be released on his own recognizance. The defense attorney's fallback position was to argue that Adam should be allowed to participate in the Brooklyn Justice Initiatives supervised release program instead of having bail set, since having bail set would inevitably mean a trip to Rikers Island.

The judge agreed to release Adam to Brooklyn Justice Initiatives instead of setting bail, which meant that Adam was required to meet with a social worker once per month and to touch base by phone twice per month while his case awaited resolution. Remaining in the community, Adam was able to keep his job in construction. He was also able to be with his young daughter when she was hospitalized for tuberculosis.

Adam maintained that he had found the bicycle on the street and was in the process of taking it to the police when he was arrested. He fully complied with the conditions of release and avoided further criminal activity. After three months on supervised release, his case was ultimately dismissed.

Brooklyn Justice Initiatives is still a work in progress. But a 2016 evaluation documented that the program has succeeded in enrolling defendants who would otherwise have faced significant bail and/or pretrial detention. Participants stayed out of jail while their cases were pending. They were also less likely to be sentenced to jail when their case was ultimately resolved.[44]

Brooklyn Justice Initiatives is just one of five supervised release programs currently operating in New York City. Taken together, these programs have the capacity to supervise three thousand defendants in the community each year. Thus far, eligibility is confined to misdemeanors and nonviolent felonies. This could soon change. Both the Lippman Commission and the mayor's office have argued that expanding supervised release is crucial to any effort to close Rikers Island. Plans are already under way to add more capacity and broaden eligibility criteria.

★   ★   ★

Anyone hoping to achieve big policy goals such as rolling back the use of incarceration or closing Rikers Island has to grapple with what will replace current practice. There is no silver bullet here. But for all the negative press that the local criminal justice system has generated of late, New York City does offer a potential roadmap for other jurisdictions to follow. The core elements include diversion programs to get low-level cases out of the system, an inclination to release defendants on their own recognizance, an investment in supervised release in lieu of bail, and a growing interest in using risk assessment tools to tailor the response to individual defendants. Add it all up and suddenly the dream of closing Rikers Island begins to look like a real possibility.

6

A CRAZY IDEA

Approximately **6** out of 10 defendants test positive for
illegal drugs at the time of their arrest[1]

It is difficult to overstate the impact of drugs on the criminal
justice system in the United States. The numbers suggest
that drugs are a contributing factor to the majority of crimes in
this country—it is estimated that six out of ten defendants test
positive for illegal drugs at the time of their arrest.[2]

Critics of the War on Drugs tend to focus on the number of
inmates who have been convicted of drug possession charges,
but the truth is that this is just the tip of the iceberg. Scratch

the surface and you will find that many crimes that have no obvious connection to drugs—shoplifting and robbery and vandalism and many more besides—are committed by individuals with substance use problems.

"If you want to understand drug addiction, go ask a municipal court judge, a local prosecutor, a hospital emergency room doctor, or *any* law enforcement professional," says General Barry McCaffrey, who was the head of the White House Office of National Drug Control Policy under President Bill Clinton. "They understand only too well, that if you're arresting people 20, 30, 40 times a year, and they've been locked up for three days, or seven days, and you turn them back out into the street with no access to treatment, for God's sakes they're back out using drugs within 12 hours. It simply doesn't work."[3]

Frontline criminal justice practitioners have been wrestling with this reality for decades, watching helplessly as drug-addicted defendants cycled through the system over and over again. Back in 1989, a small team of forward-thinking reformers in Miami, Florida, including then state attorney Janet Reno, sought to put a halt to this cycle. After some discussion and planning, they created the first-ever drug treatment court.

The idea behind the Miami drug court was simple: to offer nonviolent, drug-addicted defendants judicially monitored treatment as an alternative to prison time. By combining drug treatment with the authority of the court, the drug court sought to address the underlying problems of defendants while reducing the use of incarceration.

In truth, the Miami court was not the first to sentence a defendant to receive drug treatment. What was unique was the structure that the Miami team put in place to support defendants. First of all, they agreed that all of the eligible cases should be handled by a single judge who would receive training on the latest research about the nature of addiction and treatment. They also agreed that relapse would inevitably be part of the process for many participants. Rather than resulting in immediate termination from the program, at the Miami drug court defendants who relapsed would receive what's known in the business as "graduated sanctions"—increased drug testing, say, or more frequent reporting to court.

In addition to facing graduated sanctions, defendants could receive something even more radical: rewards. For those who successfully advanced through the stages of treatment, the drug court offered small tokens of appreciation: applause in the courtroom, journals to write in, and public recognition ceremonies. After a defendant had agreed that she wanted to participate in the program, all of the principal actors in the courtroom—judge, prosecutor, and defense attorney— worked together, taking a team approach to problems as they occurred. The drug court judge was front and center, but everyone tried to send the message that they wanted participants to succeed in treatment. Depending upon the defendant, treatment could be residential or it could be outpatient. While the court had a say in making this determination, the treatment was typically provided by a nonprofit drug program. What the court provided was a steady stream of referrals, a structure for monitoring compliance, and a powerful incentive—succeed in treatment or you could face time behind bars.

Tim Murray, of the Pretrial Justice Institute, was one of the visionaries behind the Miami drug court. "It all seems like a million years ago . . . that we launched this crazy idea where we would treat individuals as individuals," Murray remembers. "We would understand that some participants would get through the program relatively easily, while others would fail, repeatedly. That we would put forth a program that wouldn't stand as a dare for individuals to fail, but that would do everything possible to help them succeed." [4]

As conceived by Murray and others, the Miami experiment had enough unusual elements—Judges applauding defendants! Defense attorneys and prosecutors working together!—that it attracted wave after wave of international attention. When Janet Reno was named attorney general of the United States by President Bill Clinton, she brought a commitment to advancing the drug court model with her. Throughout the 1990s, drug courts began to proliferate across the United States, driven in no small part by seed funding and technical assistance provided by the U.S. Department of Justice under Reno's direction.

As drug courts spread, they also picked up political backers, both locally and at the federal level. Over the years, Congress, under both Democratic and Republican leadership, has appropriated hundreds of millions of dollars to support drug courts. Presidents Clinton, Bush, and Obama all endorsed drug courts. By combining punishment and help, drug courts managed to appeal to politicians across a fairly broad ideological spectrum. In the process, it is fair to say that drug courts helped to lay the foundation for the current bipartisan interest in criminal justice reform in this country.

A FLOURISHING INDUSTRY

Yesterday's crazy idea is today's flourishing industry. The National Association of Drug Court Professionals estimates that there are more than three thousand drug courts in operation— a reach that spreads across every U.S. state and territory.[5] Beyond federal support, there have been two principal forces that have propelled this growth.

The first is research. Drug courts are perhaps the most well-researched intervention in the history of American criminal justice reform, including multiple randomized controlled trials. A national study underwritten by the U.S. Department of Justice found reduced drug use and crime among drug court participants when compared to defendants who went through regular case processing. Drug court participants were one-third less likely to report drug use eighteen months after admission to the program. And they were responsible for less than half as many criminal acts as the comparison group.[6]

The research also suggests that drug courts are a good investment. Estimates vary, but it has been suggested that every dollar spent on drug court saves the government considerable money in reduced criminal justice expenditures. After considering how much money is saved by reduced hospital visits and the costs of future victimization, the savings can go up to as much as $27 for every drug court dollar spent.[7]

The second force propelling the expansion of drug courts has been the first-person narratives of those whose lives have been transformed. Abby Frutchey, from Machias, Maine, is one of these people. She recounted her story to *Vice* in a piece that ran with the headline, "How the Justice System Saved an Addict":

> By 17, I was drinking, smoking weed, and snorting pills plus experimenting with coke and hallucinogens. The addiction that haunted my father . . . had begun to sink its teeth into me. . . . Even an unexpected pregnancy didn't curb my use . . . they arrested me for drug trafficking . . . to my surprise, the court offered me the opportunity to enter the Washington County Adult Drug Treatment Program. . . . I didn't want to miss the next two-and-a-half years of my son's life. So I opted in. It was clear from Day One that treatment court would be nothing like what I was used to in the justice system. . . . I didn't feel like just another number on a docket. The judge, lawyers, and law enforcement

officers knew my name. . . . I successfully completed
the program in 2006 intent on maintaining my sobriety. Back in the world and no longer under court supervision, I . . . obtained my state license as a substance
use and addiction counselor. . . . Eventually, in 2012, I
was asked to serve as the treatment provider for the very
court program from which I had graduated.[8]

There are, no exaggeration, thousands of Abby Frutcheys
out there—Americans whose life trajectories have been profoundly altered for the better by their participation in drug
court and their engagement with the judges and lawyers who
staff these courts.

According to Syracuse drug court project director Kim
Kozlowski, "Part of what makes drug courts special is the human interaction with people who have a really bad disease."[9]
The human connection between defendant and judge is particularly important. Research shows that the strongest predictor of reduced future criminality is a defendant's attitude
toward the drug court judge. Strikingly, this impact is seen
across all demographics, regardless of race or gender. Even defendants with extensive prior involvement in the system were
less likely to re-offend when they perceived the judge to have
treated them fairly and respectfully.[10]

Hundreds of tough-on-crime prosecutors and judges have
been converted by their experience in drug court. "I had tried
hundreds of jury trials, prosecuted thousands upon thousands

of individuals, but I came to realize that the traditional way
of responding to the breaking of the law needed to evolve,"
reflects Thomas P. Velardi, who helms the Strafford County
Attorney's Office in Dover, New Hampshire. "I have become
known for putting tough charges and cases into the drug court,
which deals primarily with felonies."[11] J. Wesley Saint Clair,
a judge who spent time overseeing a drug court in Seattle,
Washington, offers a similar narrative: "Drug courts work,
and not because they're fuzzy—let me tell you, I can be a hard
man to deal with."[12]

Despite all of this enthusiasm, drug courts are still very
much a niche operation. A 2008 study by the Urban Institute
suggests that hundreds of thousands of addicted defendants in
the United States are not making their way into drug court.[13]
Perhaps as few as 3.8 percent of potentially treatable arrestees are participating in a drug court.[14] In a critical assessment
of drug courts, the National Association of Criminal Defense
Lawyers declared: "After 20 years, significant concerns continue to exist about the populations served by drug courts. Too
often it seems that drug court eligibility and admission criteria serve to exclude mostly indigent and minority defendants.
Drug courts must address these fundamental and disturbing
disparities. Entry requirements must be carefully considered
to ensure the same road to success is available to all."[15]

Writing in *The Atlantic*, defense attorney Emily Galvin
describes the problem this way: "Even though [drug court]

programs are available, the people who are at risk of incarceration are weeded out, for one reason or another, denied access and sent back towards the prison pipeline. For someone with a record, with a longstanding problem, ineligibility is the rule, not the exception."[16]

Sitting in her office at the Miami–Dade State Attorney's Office in 2016, Melba V. Pearson argues that increasing access to drug courts would reduce both incarceration and racial and ethnic disparities in the criminal justice system. "I firmly believe that," emphasizes Pearson, past president of the National Black Prosecutors Association. "Number one, you're receiving the services you need, so you're less likely to re-offend. And number two, it places everyone on the same playing field regardless of their [race and] financial status."[17]

But simply expanding the number of people enrolled in drug court is not enough. We must also ensure that all drug courts are good drug courts.

IMPROVING PRACTICE

In recent years, it has become clear that there are a number of areas where drug courts could improve practice. One such area is the use of medication–assisted treatment. Medications like Buprenorphine and Naltrexone have been found to block the euphoric effects of opiates, while simultaneously relieving physiological cravings and normalizing those body functions that would otherwise cause profound distress during withdrawal. "It's a game-changer," opines Kim Kozlowski, of the Syracuse drug court. "It helps people to stop thinking about seeking the drugs all the time."

Travis Bocchino, a graduate of the Syracuse drug court, attributes his sobriety to Suboxone, a form of Buprenorphine. "Suboxone's what saved my life," explains Bocchino. "I believe if you gave people that option right off the bat, got them on the Suboxone so they're not sick immediately . . . they could get their heads clear." [18] Indeed, the most comprehensive review of the research to date on drug interventions identifies medication-assisted treatment as one of the few interventions "most suitable to be included under the 'What works [to reduce recidivism]' category." [19]

Given all this, you would think that medication-assisted treatment would be part of standard operating practice at drug courts across the country. But it isn't. The reason for this is simple: many drug courts insist upon complete abstinence from all drugs. "You would think that something like this would have no natural enemies," says Kozlowski, "but there are plenty of judges who don't let [medication-assisted treatment] in a program." In the face of judges' frequent opposition to the practice, there is currently a strong push to allow defendants to utilize medication-assisted treatment in drug courts. [20] The White House Office of National Drug Control Policy has gotten involved, announcing that it would not fund drug courts that restricted access to medication-assisted treatments.

"It's really a battle between the courts and the doctors,"

says Ned Pillersdorf, an attorney who represented a Kentucky woman who was barred from taking medications to treat her addiction. "The doctor-patient relationship is sacrosanct. The courts should get out of the way."[21] From New Hampshire to Kentucky, drug courts are starting to get the message.[22]

Encouraging greater use of medication-assisted treatment is just one way that drug courts can achieve better outcomes. Another is to acknowledge and treat the prevalence of trauma and mental illness among drug court participants. When drug courts first started, mental illness and substance abuse were viewed as independent problems. According to prosecutor Thomas P. Velardi, of New Hampshire:

> Fifteen years ago, the mental health side would say, well, they have a substance abuse issue. When they get cured of their substance abuse issue, then we will treat them because it makes no sense to try to treat them while they are addicted to substance and vice versa. The substance abuse people would then say, well, they have a mental health issue. They need to be in long-term treatment for their mental health issue before they become stabilized enough to deal with their substance abuse issue. It's a complete chicken and egg [problem].

In recent years, drug courts have begun to grapple with the reality that many of their participants are dealing with serious mental health issues and histories of trauma. Judges are being trained to recognize the common signs of trauma—such as agitation, anxiety, distrust, defiance, and hostility—and understand them as coping strategies rather than character flaws. Communicating with defendants clearly and respectfully and taking an individualized approach to each case are small adjustments that judges can make to create a courtroom environment that trauma survivors will perceive as physically and emotionally safe.[23]

The focus extends to formal treatment as well. Even something as simple as asking the right questions in the right order during an eligibility screening can make an appreciable difference. Historically, drug court screening and assessment practices were narrowly focused on drug use. But individuals often start using drugs as an attempt to self-medicate or cope with a particularly trying situation. Asking a more nuanced set of questions can help clinicians uncover these kinds of connections. "Just the initial juxtaposition of questions like 'How much heroin are you using?' and 'Were you ever the victim of a crime?' starts catalyzing change," explains Victoria Dexter, of the Safe Horizon Counseling Center in Brooklyn, New York. "By up-fronting questions like that, it really is a trauma-informed approach."[24]

But perhaps the most important needed adjustment to the drug court model is increased clarity about the populations they are best suited to serve. Particularly in the early days of drug courts, there was a tendency to "cream" participants, selecting only those defendants with stable homes, supportive families, and relatively brief addiction histories. But, as we've seen, the latest research suggests that intensive interventions like drug courts are most effective when they target high-risk participants. Drug courts in New Hampshire have learned this lesson well. "We primarily accept high-risk, high-need people," explains Alex Casale, the statewide drug court coordinator. "That's the target population. All the drug courts now know that."[25]

New Hampshire's response isn't unusual. According to researcher Douglas B. Marlowe, of the National Association of Drug Court Professionals, drug courts have "embraced science like no other criminal justice program. They endorsed best practices and evidence-based practices; invited evaluators to measure their outcomes; and encouraged federal agencies . . . as well as a myriad of state agencies, to issue calls to the scientific community to closely examine the model and learn what makes it tick and how it might be improved."[26]

If drug courts should be reserved for those with the most serious addiction histories and the highest likelihood of reoffending, this raises an obvious question. Not every defendant with a drug problem meets these criteria. So what do we do with the rest?

BEYOND DRUG COURT
Judge Steven S. Alm, the creator of Hawaii's Opportunity Probation with Enforcement (HOPE) program, argues that there are some addicted defendants who don't need formal

treatment to stop using drugs. "[Many] people, in fact the majority, can stop using drugs and alcohol without going to treatment," he says. Alm contends that the use of short-term jail (often just a day or two) as a punishment for failed drug tests is often all it takes: "If they know there's going to be a jail sanction for every violation, most of the folks stop." [27]

As Alm suggests, the HOPE model is based on one central insight: that the swiftness and certainty of punishment is more important to behavioral change than the length or harshness of a sanction. In practice, the HOPE model relies on judges to communicate clearly to participants the precise consequences that will be imposed for probation violations. In the event of such a violation, the consequences are imposed immediately and consistently. This is a sea change from standard practice, where probation violations tend to go unaddressed until enough accrue for a judge to bring down the hammer and send the probationer back to jail. One national study explains the effect: "Offenders . . . are willing to roll the dice with repeated violations of probation when the consequences are delayed and uncertain. . . . [They] are far less likely to risk going to jail today even for a single violation . . . when in HOPE Probation. The logic of HOPE Probation is that clear and easily understood rules are more readily followed by offenders." [28]

Treatment is available in HOPE, but as Alm describes, probationers who think they can succeed without it are afforded the opportunity to do so: "They say, 'Judge, it's been six months. I think I can stop on my own.' I say, 'Great, but you're going to have to show us that by coming in and testing clean.'" Thus far, the HOPE model has received a mix of positive and negative reviews in the empirical literature.[29] But federal funders like the National Institute of Justice and the Bureau of Justice Assistance have seen enough that they have been convinced to spread the model. Today, at least forty jurisdictions across eighteen states have implemented a version of HOPE.[30]

HOPE and drug court are appropriate alternatives for those individuals facing serious jail or prison time. But experience tells us that thousands of individuals struggling with addiction are arrested for minor, quality-of-life offenses. These people should not receive long probation or treatment sentences. In fact, some of them probably shouldn't be coming to court at all. Recognizing this reality, innovative police chiefs and prosecutors across the country have begun to launch drug diversion programs. Seattle Law Enforcement Assisted Diversion, better known as LEAD, is an example.

In LEAD, officers in Seattle, Washington, have the option of connecting individuals with addiction problems directly to service providers rather than booking them into the jail. Participants avoid formal arrest and court involvement altogether. LEAD takes a "guerilla approach" to service provision. LEAD case managers are trained to engage clients with profoundly unstable lives. This includes visiting clients at home and accompanying them to appointments.[31] Voluntary engagement is integral to the program's success, and this means—above all—treating participants with dignity and respect. "They don't look at you like you're a waste of money, and they don't look at you like you're a crazy crackhead that needs to go somewhere. They actually look at you like you're a person," reflects one LEAD participant.[32]

Alongside drug addiction, the typical LEAD participant faces numerous other challenges, including high rates of homelessness and serious mental illness. Local prosecutor Mary Barbosa acknowledges that success for a participant in LEAD can be relative: "Maybe they're going to the ER [emergency room] once a month instead of four times a month—that's still progress."[33] Nonetheless, research to date does show that LEAD participants are significantly less likely to be rearrested than those in a control group.[34]

Programs like LEAD and HOPE and drug court have both practical and symbolic value. They send a message not just to participants, but to criminal justice officials and the broader public as well, that the standard approach to substance abuse is not working. "I think it's really changed the attitude of police as far as how do you best deploy your resources," notes Police Captain Marcus Williams, from Seattle. "Do you spend your time continuing booking people in jail for small offenses, or do you try and engage them in something different than what you've been doing for a long time that isn't working?"[35] Dan Satterberg, Seattle's prosecuting attorney, puts the matter even more succinctly: "If you try to help people on the margins of society, it turns out you have better luck than if you punish them."[36]

7

CHALLENGING POPULATIONS

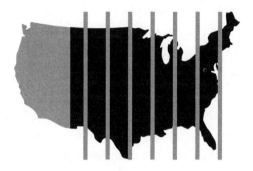

About **75 percent** of the defendants convicted of a felony were sentenced to incarceration in a state prison or local jail[1]

Even after reducing its population from 22,000 to 17,000 inmates in recent years, the Los Angeles County jail system remains the largest in the United States.[2] It houses an inmate population that is "one of the most complex and criminally-entrenched in the nation," according to Captain Paula Tokar, of the Los Angeles County Sheriff's Department. In Los Angeles, the vast majority of misdemeanor defendants are released on a promise to appear at arraignment, as are those with outstanding bail amounts totaling less than

$25,000. This leaves a jail population charged with more serious offenses.[3] And this leads to a simple truth: in Los Angeles, significantly reducing the use of jail will not be possible if decision-makers are not comfortable providing alternatives for felony-level defendants.

Los Angeles County District Attorney Jackie Lacey understands this reality. She argues that "not all felonies are created equal," and that many individuals charged with felonies are good candidates for diversion.[4] This truth extends far beyond Los Angeles: if the goal is to considerably reduce the use of jail and prison in the United States, alternatives to incarceration cannot be limited to lower-level offenses and offenders.

Talking about alternatives to incarceration for felony-level defendants isn't always a popular cause.[5] Consequently, many reform efforts have excluded defendants charged with more serious offenses and those who have prior convictions for violent felonies.[6]

But felony-level diversion can be successful precisely because the stakes are high—the threat of a felony charge can provide plenty of personal motivation for defendants. And the social science is clear that higher-risk defendants benefit the most—in terms of recidivism reduction—from intensive interventions.[7]

Like a growing number of prosecutors, Jackie Lacey is not convinced that business as usual is working: "Our recidivism rates are high. That, to me, means we're failing. If we're imprisoning people and then letting people out and they're back in a short period of time, that's not a success."

Lacey is the first African American, and the first woman, to serve as Los Angeles district attorney. Her commitment to community-based alternatives to incarceration is personal: "I embrace diversion because I came from a background where, there but for the grace of God go I. I had relatives, friends who became addicted to drugs and went off on a different path. They were just as smart as I was, just as talented, but for whatever reason got waylaid at an early age into that culture."

It can be a challenge to marshal public sympathies for those who have been charged with felony-level crimes, particularly those that involve violence. A civilized society depends upon a condemnation of violent behavior. We look to the criminal justice system, and judges and prosecutors in particular, to help deliver this condemnation. Even when defendants have sympathetic backstories, many judges and prosecutors often feel reluctant to take a risk in felony cases. Their concerns are understandable: the local media (and elected officials) are typically all too happy to second-guess a release decision that ends in violence. Many criminal justice officials are reluctant to expose themselves to this kind of scrutiny.

But not all. Lacey is one of a growing number of prosecutors who are beginning to take a deeper look at the people behind the cases on their dockets. These prosecutors are coming to acknowledge a complicated reality: contrary to our childhood games, it is not so easy to divide the world into "good guys" and "bad guys." Today's perpetrator is yesterday's victim. And vice versa.

All felony-level offenders merit attention, but in recent years three populations have been the focus of special reform efforts: defendants struggling with mental illness, those who have committed domestic violence offenses, and those who straddle the nebulous line between late adolescence and early adulthood. Coming up with meaningful interventions for these populations is crucial to reducing the use of incarceration in the United States. Thankfully, we are not starting from scratch—a number of programs already in place show that it may be possible to keep many of these individuals in the community rather than locking them up behind bars.

A BLESSING IN DISGUISE

Jevon is a case in point. The police found Jevon in a psychotic state at a New York City park. He had forty-six bags of crack cocaine in his possession. Jevon was forty-two years old at the time. He had previously been arrested on several occasions for selling pirated DVDs on the subway. "He was probably symptomatic for a long time," explains Katie Herman, a social worker at the Center for Alternative Sentencing and Employment Services (CASES), an alternative-to-incarceration program in New York City. "But he wouldn't be yelling and screaming on the street. I assume that no one really knew what was going on until he came into our program."[8]

Jevon says he started using drugs two years prior to the arrest, including cocaine, synthetic marijuana ("K2"), and cannabis ("Purple Haze"), which triggered hallucinations. As far as he can remember, Jevon had never received any mental health treatment.

Jevon was charged with criminal possession of a controlled substance—a felony. He spent months on Rikers Island in pretrial detention. It was a harrowing experience. "I've seen inmates throw hot water in other inmates' faces. I've seen [guards] beat inmates. I've seen inmates try to commit suicide," he reports.[9] Jevon's experience highlights another simple truth: jails are not typically designed with the stability of mentally ill inmates in mind. The violence, isolation, and uncertainty all can take their toll. "The experience of incarceration can often exacerbate existing symptoms of mental illness or serve as a stressor that triggers new psychiatric episodes," says Virginia Barber-Rioja, a clinical instructor of psychiatry at New York University.[10]

With the assistance of his defense attorney, Jevon was eventually admitted to a special program that CASES runs for adults with serious mental illness. The program is a twenty-four-hour-a-day, seven-days-a-week operation. Recognizing the complex needs of its participants, the program goes well beyond the typical office- or clinic-based approach to the provision of treatment and services. "It's a different way of providing both treatment and supervision in a model that's completely mobile," explains Ann-Marie Louison, of CASES.

"It is about engaging the client in the community, in their natural setting, so the structure is created by the team going out and delivering the service rather than the four walls of a residential treatment setting." [11]

The CASES team includes psychiatrists, nurses, and social workers. Together, they seek to address a client's full range of social service needs. "If they're homeless, then the team helps with housing. If they don't have benefits, the team works to establish all those things, at the same time addressing any of the treatment issues related to their diagnoses," says Bradley Jacobs, of CASES. [12] In other words, CASES has found that simply addressing a client's mental health issues in isolation is not sufficient; to truly be effective, service providers must be multifaceted.

This was certainly the case with Jevon. Jevon needed counseling. He also needed help with his drug problem and a place to live. Just solving one of these problems would not have sufficed. Luckily, over the course of numerous interactions, Jevon accessed group counseling, medication management, and housing assistance. His situation stabilized.

Jevon is hardly the only vulnerable individual to spend time in New York City jails. Indeed, it is estimated that 11 percent of the jail population suffers from a serious mental illness, while 42 percent have a mental health diagnosis of some kind. [13] The tragic case of Kalief Browder, the young man who committed suicide after years of abuse and solitary confinement on Rikers

Island, has come to symbolize the harms that jail can do to those struggling with mental health issues.

Another defendant with mental health issues, Cruz, could easily have been another Kalief Browder. A judge had found Cruz unfit to proceed at trial after being charged with making bomb threats to radio stations he says were playing music that had been stolen from him. According to Cruz: "I had no idea that I was . . . having mental health issues, I was actually acting out somewhat, beyond a little bit of my control. I took some steps that were outside of the law, that were illegal. Eventually, like a blessing in disguise, the legal authorities, they caught up with me."[14] Cruz says he started using drugs at the age of nine or ten after being sexually abused by an uncle. "I didn't have the capacity to go and tell my mother or tell my family. It all stayed like a secret within me," Cruz recalls. "Then, out in the street, I started smoking marijuana." Luckily Cruz, like Jevon, was admitted to CASES.

Participants in the program, like Cruz and Jevon, are typically facing a prison sentence of four to five years. "The majority of our clients have pretty long criminal records," says social worker Katie Herman. The most common charge is attempted assault. To participate in the program, defendants must plead guilty to a felony charge. Their sentence is deferred while they are engaged in the program. All successful participants avoid prison time.

Both Jevon and Cruz did well at CASES, avoiding re-arrest

and hospitalization. The first outcome is consistent with the program's overall track record: since 2013, no graduate of the program has accrued a new felony conviction in the two years following completion.[15] But the latter outcome—avoiding hospitalization—is less typical. "A lot of our clients will go off their medication and they need to go to the hospital a lot," explains Herman.

After nearly two and a half years in the program, Jevon successfully completed his court mandate and was sentenced to three years of probation. "CASES helped me a lot," he says. "If CASES wasn't available, I would probably still be in jail—probably be dead. They helped me a lot. Helped me get back on the right path with my life."

"CASES has done incredible things for me," echoes Cruz. He successfully completed his court mandate and was sentenced to a conditional discharge, thereby avoiding both prison and a felony conviction on his permanent record.

This success has not gone unnoticed. In 2016, New York City invested in a fivefold expansion of the CASES program.[16] "What began as a recognition of the correlation between untreated mental illness and incarceration and recidivism," reflects CASES president Joel Copperman, "has led to a commitment by government to ensure that an especially high-risk population has the support they need to avoid incarceration and succeed in the community." [17] Nationally, similar models have been implemented in Rochester, Chicago, and the

California Central Valley, resulting in decreased jail and inpatient hospital days.[18]

BETWEEN IMPULSE AND ACTION

Many of the programs attempting to effect behavioral change among defendants with mental health issues employ cognitive-behavioral therapy.[19] Research shows that cognitive-behavioral therapy can be effective in reducing recidivism, particularly among higher-risk individuals.[20]

Robert Hindman is a clinical psychologist at the Beck Institute, one of the premier postgraduate training institutes for therapists. For Hindman, the most fundamental tenet of cognitive-behavioral therapy is this: "It's not the situation that leads to our reactions, it's our interpretation of the situation."[21] He often uses the example of a missed text message to explain this idea:

You text a friend or a family member, and it's two hours later and you haven't heard back. I ask, "What's your reaction going to be?" Most people say, "Oh, you know, I'd be so angry." I then ask, "Okay, what would go through your mind to lead you to feel angry?" They'll say, "Oh, you know, that they're ignoring me." I'm like, "Okay. What could be another interpretation of why they're taking this long to respond?" They may say something like, "Maybe they're busy." I'm like, "Okay.

If you think they're busy, then what's your reaction going to be?" They'll say, "Oh well, I might be a little annoyed," or "I might just feel pretty neutral." Okay, then I'll ask, "Let's say you feel anxious when they haven't responded. What might be going through your mind?" They'll say, "That they might be hurt or they've been in an accident." This example shows them how it's the exact same situation—you've texted the person and they haven't responded in a few hours. But what drives the emotion and behavior is what your interpretation of the situation is.

The goal of cognitive-behavioral therapy is to develop an awareness of how reactions affect behavior—and then help clients adopt a different set of responses. "It's trying to get a little space between the impulse and the action," explains Hindman.

Cognitive-behavioral therapy is a tool that is valuable for anyone seeking to gain a better understanding—and better sense of control—of their actions. But it is particularly valuable for those who have engaged in criminal behavior. Hindman describes how he works with those who have engaged in violent behavior:

They might say something like, "Well, I have to protect myself. If I'm not going to be aggressive toward other people, if I don't assault people, then I'm going to look weak and I'm going to be attacked more." When this urge or impulse shows up, all they think about is the reasons why they should [fight]. They don't really consider the reasons why not to. If you can get to those reasons why they shouldn't, the disadvantages, and get them to remind themselves of those in the moment, they can stop themselves from going ahead with the behavior.

A prime example of cognitive-behavioral therapy in action is a program called Thinking for a Change, which is often used in American correctional settings.[22] "I would say the heart of [Thinking for a Change] . . . is cognitive self-change," says Juliana Taymans, one of the creators of the program. "[I]t is up to the offender to identify, to look at his thinking, identify key risk thoughts, feelings, attitudes, and beliefs, and to connect them to what he does."[23]

Thinking for a Change teaches participants a range of skills to assist them in avoiding future involvement with the criminal justice system. For example, participants practice how to identify and modify their thinking in stressful situations, such as a conflict with their boss at work. They also work on basic social skills like active listening and negotiating.[24] The program wraps up with participants moving sequentially through problem solving from "Stop and Think" (recognizing they are having a problem), all the way to "Do and Evaluate" (trying out a nonharmful action). Participants are strongly encouraged to practice these skills outside of the group. "The whole idea is that you're using these skills in your real life," underscores Taymans, "so you need some time to run into situations where you might be able to use the skills."

It takes resources to implement Thinking for a Change—and stamina to complete the program. It is a closed group intervention, meaning that no additional participants can join after the first session. It takes a minimum of twenty-seven sessions to finish the program. Facilitators are advised to limit the group size to twelve participants, which means that there is no place for reluctant participants to hide.[25]

Thinking for a Change is currently used in about forty-five states.[26] Research indicates that Thinking for a Change can increase pro-social attitudes and skills and reduce recidivism among felony-level populations.[27] The National Institute of Corrections is committed to increasing the use of Thinking for a Change, having already trained more than ten thousand individuals to serve as group facilitators.[28] "It's a very commonsense curriculum," reflects Holly Busby, of the National Institute of Corrections. "That's why we continue to support it, to fund it. We're getting an increasing number of requests from the field."[29]

Busby emphasizes that Thinking for a Change is not the answer for all offenders: "It's not a magic fix . . . it takes ongoing commitment and supervision for agencies to actually see the true effect over a long period of time." Indeed, Thinking for a Change isn't the only model out there.[30] More important than the type of cognitive-behavioral program is the quality of the program itself.[31] If a cognitive-behavioral program is well implemented—with well-trained staff and the right participants—the evidence suggests that it will make a difference. Not a huge difference, perhaps, but a difference nonetheless. For example, a recent study documents that if an individual had a 40 percent likelihood of re-offending, cognitive-behavioral programing lowered it on average to 30 percent.

IDENTIFYING VALUES

Intimate partner violence occurs all too frequently in the United States. It is estimated that millions of Americans are abused by an intimate partner each year—and this is almost certainly an undercount, given the hidden and unreported nature of this crime.[32]

In many states, individuals convicted of assault against an intimate partner are required to attend a batterer intervention program. Unfortunately, none of the most popular batterer intervention programs has been documented to reduce recidivism significantly.[33]

Frustrated with the existing models, many places are starting to explore alternatives. One such place is the state of Iowa.

In 2009, the Iowa Department of Corrections approached the University of Iowa for assistance in developing a new program model. "Just like every other jurisdiction, we were not getting good outcomes," recalls Sally Kreamer, of the Iowa

Department of Corrections. "We made a decision that we were going to try to develop something else that we could pilot."[34] At that same moment, a doctoral candidate at the University of Iowa, Amie Zarling, was testing a new treatment for domestic violence offenders.

"It was really an act of bravery, a leap of faith," reflects Zarling, who is now a professor at Iowa State University. Zarling created a new batterer intervention curriculum—Achieving Change Through Value-Based Behavior or "ACTV." According to Zarling: "The men responded very well to it. So then we did a statewide training. . . . That was in 2010–2011, and since then it has spread like wildfire."[35]

The ACTV program unfolds over the course of twenty-four sessions and five skills-based modules. Facilitator Elaine Bales elaborates: "[Participants] do not have to sit down and do a whole reciting of their criminal history or whatever the event was that brought them here. We don't even talk about the incident that got them put into the program. In the [previous model], they had to admit that they had done it, and it started them right off the bat being very defensive. That was probably the biggest switch [in approach]."[36] The ACTV program addresses a range of "barriers to change," from substance abuse to parenting struggles to unemployment.[37] As with some cognitive-behavioral therapies, Zarling emphasizes the importance of "mindfulness," teaching participants a form of awareness to help them avoid the habitual rush to judgment: "The first step is becoming aware of your inner experiences, which are your thoughts, your emotions, any urges or sensations that you have."

For Bales, who has to manage a room full of men accused of domestic violence, mindfulness is critical. "We talk about it in terms of giving yourself some wiggle room, giving yourself some space," explains Bales, "getting off of autopilot."

The critical step is identifying values. According to Zarling, "We basically assist the men in identifying what is most important to them in life." She explains: "Our biggest fear at the beginning of this was that they would not have prosocial values. However, 99.9 percent of the time, these men have values. Number one is probably their kids if they have kids. Family. Spirituality. Work. A lot of them have just never been asked what's important to them, and then a lot of them don't know how to live a life in service of those values."[38] This emphasis on values helps participants connect the various skills that are taught throughout the program with the need to make changes and reduce harmful behaviors.

According to Sally Kreamer, of the Iowa Department of Corrections, "We're seeing good results for offenders that have been really hard to deal with." Specifically, new research out of Iowa shows that the ACTV model can reduce recidivism generally, and domestic assaults specifically. To assess the intervention, Zarling and her colleagues compared the outcomes of men assigned to the ACTV program to those who went to the regular batterer intervention program. According to Zarling: "Men who completed ACTV had half the rates of general re-offense within one year compared to men who went through the treatment-as-usual program. If you look specifically at domestic violence, it reduced by two-thirds: 14 percent of men who completed treatment-as-usual re-offended with a domestic assault charge within one year compared to only five percent of men who went through ACTV." [39] Zarling also found an overall reduction in violent crime: "We collapsed all violent charges together, not just domestic violence, but also child abuse, armed robbery—any violent charge. Eight percent of men who completed ACTV had a re-offense for any violent charge compared to 23 percent of men who completed treatment-as-usual." [40]

The news wasn't all positive: those in the ACTV group were less likely to complete the program than those in the standard batterer intervention program. [41] Lettie Prell, director of research with the Iowa Department of Corrections, hypothesizes that the lower completion rate likely reflects the intensity of the intervention: "In ACTV . . . men are required to be engaged in the learning experience." [42]

Moving forward, Zarling is working with other jurisdictions that are interested in replicating the model, including the state of Vermont. The Vermont Department of Corrections began searching for a new batterer intervention model in 2012. "Our [existing] curriculum had an extremely heavy focus on having [participants] recite what they did," explains Kim Bushey, of the Vermont Department of Corrections.

"The reality is the evidence doesn't support that admission has any correlation with re-offending."[43]

Heather Holter, of the Vermont Council on Domestic Violence, hopes the ACTV pilot might be the start of broader change in Vermont: "I would love to see us someday get to a point where we really are using risk assessment . . . to figure out who needs to be incarcerated because they are truly dangerous, and who really needs programming because they just do not have the skills to change the damaging behavior that they have just become so entrenched in."[44]

PROCLIVITY FOR RISK

The ACTV model seeks to reduce a specific set of negative behaviors (domestic abuse) by changing the way that participants think. It has recently become clear that not all offenders think alike. Indeed, some people are particularly bad at weighing the consequences of their actions. This is often the case for young people.

In general, the law recognizes that young minds work differently than adult minds. For example, the U.S. Supreme Court has put an end to capital punishment and mandatory life imprisonment without parole for juveniles, declaring that adolescence is marked by "rashness, proclivity for risk, and inability to assess consequences."[45] Using similar logic, almost every state in the United States has established that the age of criminal responsibility generally begins at eighteen;

defendants who have not yet reached this threshold are adjudicated in special courts that are designed to serve the best interests of the child.

None of this is new news. What is new is neurological research that strongly suggests that the period of adolescence actually extends well beyond the teenage years into early adulthood. Specifically, the development of the prefrontal cortex—the part of the brain that regulates functions like impulse control and reasoning—can continue up until around the age of twenty-four. This means that many eighteen- to twenty-four-year-olds possess a range of characteristics that encourage law-breaking—risky and impulsive behaviors, an orientation to immediate rewards rather than long-term thinking and emotional volatility.[46] "People are not magically different on their 18th birthday," notes Columbia University law professor Elizabeth Scott. "Their brains are still maturing, and the criminal justice system should find a way to take that into account."[47]

The implications of this insight are potentially far-reaching. Young people between the ages of eighteen and twenty-four make up roughly a quarter of all prison admissions in the United States. This is a group that commits a lot of offenses. But it is also a group that may be particularly amenable to rehabilitation. According to Vincent Schiraldi, of Harvard University, "They're the least culpable and most malleable people left in the adult system."[48]

In order to help them transition to law-abiding, adult life, the criminal justice system must understand the unique challenges and opportunities that young adults present and adapt itself accordingly. Of course, the idea that the system might treat eighteen- to twenty-four-year-olds more like adolescents than adults can be a tough sell. Nancy Campbell, who has consulted with corrections agencies throughout the country for over twenty-five years, cites a glaring paucity of programs for this group. "I have been in this business long enough that it saddens me to see that we are not further along," she reflects. "We are such a bloody punitive culture."[49]

What would a better, less punitive approach look like? Advocates like Schiraldi have called for the justice system to stop charging young people as adults, to stop saddling them with lifelong criminal records, and to stop housing them in correctional facilities alongside older inmates. They have also argued for specialized courts and probation programs that would link participants to mental health and trauma assessments and positive opportunities to develop life and job skills.

"SOMEONE THAT WANTS TO HELP"

It will be a long time before the criminal justice system can reorient itself in this direction. Meanwhile, in the here and now, thousands of emerging adults continue to flood into the justice system. Probation officer Alvin Cole, who works in Des Moines, Iowa, offers the example of David, a nineteen-year-old who was sentenced to probation for carrying a weapon and for assault.[50] Cole reports that David had a rough childhood that included a period of incarceration in a juvenile correctional facility. His father was incarcerated for gang-related activities, and as a child David witnessed multiple family members get shot. Cole recalls his initial impressions of David: "He got involved with the wrong people, made a bad decision, and didn't have any support system out here. He reminded me of myself when I decided to come out here to work—just not having any connections and not knowing what to do when you're in a new area."

David was on probation for two years. He was required to participate in an intensive cognitive-behavioral treatment group, co-facilitated by Cole. He was also required to attend high school—he eventually graduated and is planning to attend college. In addition to closely monitoring his whereabouts and compliance, Cole invested a lot of time in David, pushing him to succeed:

> What we try to do is not make it feel for the client like an assembly-line type of system. I work with clients on a daily basis, having conversations about their lives, conversations about what they plan to do and how to do it. It helps make things a bit more natural where the client can feel more comfortable and open up a bit more. I try to have conversations with the clients so that they understand, "Hey, I want you to see me as someone that wants to help as opposed to someone that wants to ultimately lock you up."

Although the program strongly encourages family members and other significant people to participate in supporting their loved ones, David didn't have anyone to lean on. Cole made efforts to get him connected to a positive support system. There were certainly bumps along the way, including a few missed appointments. But David did not commit any new crimes during his two years on probation.

In the end, David's success hinged on some elements that are unique to his age—the support to make it through high school and the mentoring role that Cole played probably would not have been necessary with an older probationer. But other elements of David's story are simply good practice, regardless of age; this includes the use of cognitive-behavioral therapy and the presence of a caring authority figure. Almost no one transforms their life without these kinds of services and connections.

★   ★   ★

The reforms that we have described in this chapter offer the basic outlines of how we might begin to handle more felony-level offenders in the community. We must invest in programs that focus on changing behavior by giving participants new ways to think and new tools for dealing with conflict. We must give these programs the resources they need so that they can create small group settings that allow for intensive work with participants and encourage individual accountability. And we must spread the use of good risk assessment tools so that the right participants can be matched to the right interventions.

We should not kid ourselves: going down this path won't be easy. It will cost money. It will require some measure of courage on the part of the prosecutors and judges and probation officers who make decisions about what happens with individual defendants. And it will demand patience and understanding from the media, elected officials, and the general public, who must have realistic expectations about what alternatives to incarceration can deliver in terms of results.

But the good news is that the programs in Vermont and Iowa and New York that we have profiled just scratch the surface. There are dozens of social service innovators across the country who are showing that it is possible to keep challenging defendant populations in the community—and to do so in ways that are safe, effective, and, above all, humane.

8

STATES OF CHANGE

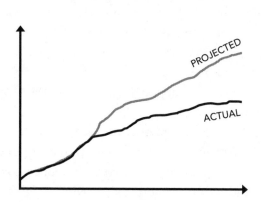

Georgia's prison system has about **8,000** fewer inmates than was projected for 2017[1]

When Republican governor Nathan Deal took office in January 2011, Georgia's prison population was still growing; the corrections budget had already reached $1 billion per year. "I was told that as Governor, I should be prepared to build two new adult prisons because our prison population would grow by another 5,000 during my first term," recalls Deal, a former prosecutor.[2] One in three adults was returning to prison within three years of release from confinement. (The recidivism rate was even higher for juveniles.)[3] Without intervention, the prison population was projected to reach close to sixty thousand by the year 2016, with an additional $264 million required to accommodate the increase.[4] According to Governor Deal, "The most alarming statistic was the large number of prisoners who were classified as 'non-violent.' Most of those 'non-violent' prisoners had substance abuse problems." Low-risk drug and property offenders accounted for 25 percent of all individuals sentenced to the Georgia Department of Corrections.[5]

Georgia is not alone in its efforts to analyze the future trajectory of its criminal justice system. In recent years, dozens of states have sought to simultaneously reduce correctional spending and improve public safety. Much of this work has been driven by something known as the Justice Reinvestment Initiative. The idea behind justice reinvestment is simple: to encourage administrative and legislative changes at the state level that will result in significant cost savings in terms of reduced spending on corrections. These savings can then be "reinvested" in community-based rehabilitative programs.

The idea behind justice reinvestment might be straightforward, but the implementation is not. It involves all three branches of government agreeing to work together. It requires intensive data analysis. And it demands a commitment to bipartisan political consensus. To help states interested in embarking down this path, nonprofit groups, including the Council of State Governments and the Pew Charitable Trusts, provide research support and strategic advice, much of it underwritten by the U.S. Department of Justice.

"The fact that we were ultimately able to [institute change] in Georgia, a state that has legislative and executive branches run by Republicans, makes for a pretty interesting conversation about the soundness of smart-on-crime policy reform initiatives," notes Georgia Supreme Court Justice Michael P. Boggs.[6] In 2012, Boggs was appointed by Governor Deal to serve as co-chair of the Criminal Justice Reform Council, a group charged with finding problems to solve within the criminal justice system that might yield to bipartisan consensus. The first problem the council chose to tackle was drug crime.

Justice Boggs had witnessed the potential of alternatives to incarceration firsthand, having once presided over a felony-level drug court in Georgia. Even those without a personal connection were won over when they reviewed the research literature, which credited adult drug courts with appreciable reductions in both recidivism and drug use. Several studies documented even larger effects for higher-risk individuals and users of more serious drugs (for example, heroin and cocaine).[7]

The Criminal Justice Reform Council recommended expanded funding for drug courts and other specialized "accountability courts" in Georgia. "We've not only expanded the number of accountability courts but we've enlarged the scope," explains Boggs. "We are now increasing the number of veterans' courts, family dependency courts, DUI courts, mental health courts, and of course adult felony drug courts." Georgia's accountability courts now have the capacity to serve upwards of 3,500 participants each year.[8]

The council did not stop there. It also moved to a weight-based classification scheme for drug crimes. This new approach sought to reduce stays in prison for those convicted of possession of smaller amounts of drugs. It also sought to increase the number of individuals who would be deemed eligible for an accountability court program.

The decision to start with drug crimes in Georgia was strategic. "By focusing on this segment of our prison population first, we proved that there was a better way," explains Governor Deal. He adds that the success of this initial reform effort paved the way for a more expansive and ambitious approach to rethinking incarceration in Georgia:

> That allowed us to move into some of the more difficult areas of criminal justice reform: community-based diversion programs for juveniles; reforms within our prison system which focused on increasing educational and technical skills of inmates; establishing a Department of Transition Support and Re-Entry to reduce our recidivism rate; and consolidating our Parole Supervisors, Probation Officers, and Juvenile Probation Officers under a new Department of Community Supervision, which eliminated gaps in our services and allowed our resources to be used more efficiently.

All of these moves were accomplished with bipartisan support. According to Zoë Towns, of the Pew Charitable Trusts, the ultimate impact was dramatic: "In a state like Georgia, the governor put the brakes on forty years of very fast, very steep growth in the prison population." The numbers suggest that Georgia has indeed succeeded in bending the curve, significantly altering the projected growth in the state prison population. As we write this, Georgia's prison system has about eight thousand fewer inmates than was projected for 2017.[9] And the number of African Americans committed to Georgia prisons had dropped to roughly ten thousand from more than thirteen thousand in 2009.[10]

That said, the number of Georgians behind bars is essentially the same today as it was in 2009.[11] Years of effort and energy by really smart and committed people have altered Georgia's trajectory, but they have not dramatically reduced the number of people behind bars.

So what are we to take away from the Georgia experience? The most important lesson is that reducing incarceration in the United States is not going to happen overnight. Reformers in Georgia have devoted an enormous amount of time, money, and political capital to the cause of reform. They have found that the criminal justice system changes course slowly, if it changes course at all.

PULLING OFF THE BAND-AID

Mississippi was inspired, not daunted, by the Georgia story.

There were compelling reasons for Mississippi's interest in criminal justice reform. In 2012, 717 out of every 100,000 people in the state of Mississippi were in prison.[12] "Mississippi was second in the nation in incarceration rates," recalls Mississippi state senator Brice Wiggins. "This was a response, like many states, to the tough-on-crime policies that were put into place in the early nineties."[13] For example, in 1995, a "truth in sentencing" law abolished parole in Mississippi and reduced possible earned release time, effectively requiring all inmates to serve at least 85 percent of their sentences in prison.[14]

A self-described "strong on crime" Republican, Senator Wiggins came to believe that Mississippi's approach to incarceration was failing on multiple fronts: "What people need to understand is that this led to essentially a bankrupting of the state . . . it was [also] a family values issue. . . . When somebody goes to prison, it not only affects that person, but it affects their family. It's hard on the kids."

Digging into the data is a key piece of the justice reinvestment approach, so that's exactly what Wiggins and other decision-makers in Mississippi did. What they found alarmed them. According to Wiggins, approximately 85 percent of the sentenced population in Mississippi was on probation. Another 15 percent was incarcerated. But state budget allocations were essentially reversed: in 2013, the Mississippi Department of Corrections budget was $360 million, of which only $26 million was directed to community supervision.[15]

Moreover, the numbers suggested that roughly three out of four people were admitted to prison in Mississippi for nonviolent offenses.[16] "We saw people serving ten, twenty, and thirty years for nonviolent offenses," says Jody Owens II, who leads the Southern Poverty Law Center's Mississippi office.[17]

As in Georgia, drug-related crime was widespread in Mississippi. "Unfortunately, almost everybody's had a family member hit with drugs or something like that," says Wiggins. Among other things, this meant more and more individuals and families exposed to the conditions of confinement in Mississippi. According to Owens, "[Mississippi prisons] are bad. Horrible things are happening to people. We have families to this day that are still paying for protection for their child or their brother or husband inside of a prison. If they don't pay weekly, whether it be a money order or something, they get pictures of their family member's face beat up, blood all over them, or someone calls them crying. What's happening in these places was just ridiculous."

In 2014, Mississippi enacted a comprehensive package of sentencing and corrections reforms—"In essence, we pulled off the whole Band-Aid," remarks Senator Wiggins. Among other things, the legislation increased access to alternatives to incarceration and standardized the parole release process. In particular, lawmakers sought to limit the use of prison beds to violent and career offenders.

Although there was strong support for the reforms in Mississippi, including endorsements from the Mississippi Association of Chiefs of Police and the state prosecutors' association, there were also dissenters. "Basically, you'll never, ever go to jail if you steal somebody's stuff," said State Representative Mark Baker, who voted against the measures. "Without that stick out there, crime runs rampant." [18]

A number of key players helped to overcome critics like Baker. One of the most important was Andy Gipson, perhaps the most conservative member of the Mississippi House of Representatives. "I will admit, I was skeptical going into this whole process," reflects Gipson.[19] He describes a change of mind:

> Everybody knew about the tremendous cost that our prison system was just continually escalating here in Mississippi. We were at one point the second highest budget item right behind our education budget and growing rapidly every day. The one thing that got my attention as a rather conservative member of the House of Representatives is the results that we were seeing for those costs were abysmal because you had people on average re-offending within three years of being released. That didn't make any sense from a fiscal standpoint.

He also describes a change of heart:

> I am a Christian. I am a believer. That's a strong common bond that we have in Mississippi for all the things that might divide us otherwise. I think our faith really unifies the people of the State of Mississippi across the board. We heard from faith-based stakeholders who said, "This is an opportunity to help people really change the direction not only of their lives, but their families' lives, and the legacy that they're going to leave; to give them a second chance, to turn what is a bad situation, not only for themselves but for their families, into a really transformational return of that person back to society in a productive way."

Like Wiggins, Gipson attributes a lot of his—and his constituents'—support for alternatives to incarceration to the effects of drug use on families. He also points to a lack of public trust—particularly among victims of crime—in the criminal justice system resulting from inconsistent incarceration practices. "Nobody involved in corrections in Mississippi . . . could tell how long any offender, whether they were violent or nonviolent, was actually going to spend behind bars," explains Gipson. "You had people being sentenced for the same crime, in different jurisdictions, one might serve ten years in prison, the other would get out earlier."

Another problem in Mississippi was the reality that many

individuals were being admitted to prison for violating parole, probation, or other supervision programs—over a third of the prison population was incarcerated because of a supervision revocation.[20] This is not an uncommon problem. Across the country, many people find themselves behind bars not because they have committed a crime, but because they have violated the terms of their probation or parole—violating curfews, missing appointments, failing drug tests. "We know from the research that swift and certain and proportional responses are better at curbing offending behavior than random, delayed, and severe ones," observes Zoë Towns, of the Pew Charitable Trusts. "What we saw in the Mississippi probation and parole system was random, delayed, and severe sanctions." What this means in real terms is that the system would not respond to multiple violations by a parolee or a probationer. Then, when enough misbehavior had added up, the system would go immediately to its most punitive reaction: incarceration. The social science on behavior modification is pretty clear that this is the wrong way to go. At a minimum, Mississippi was missing multiple opportunities to correct misbehavior through more modest (and less expensive) interventions—electronic monitoring, more frequent reporting, and curfews, for example.

The reform package in Mississippi sought to solve problems by standardizing sanctions for probation and parole violations. In the process, efforts were made to promote the use of graduated responses to earlier and less-serious violations. Crucially, lawmakers in Mississippi applied all of the changes they were making retroactively. This contributed to a significant drop in the state's prison population—from 21,367 in 2011 to 18,789 in 2015.[21]

The experience in Georgia and Mississippi suggests that reducing prison populations is rarely a straight-line process: sometimes two steps forward are followed by a step backward. The reform process is subject to the dynamics of local politics, personalities, and culture, any of which can derail even the most committed change agents.

There is still much work to be done in Mississippi, of course. But it is safe to say that if change is possible in Mississippi, a state that for many symbolizes the worst of the American justice system, there is hope that reform can take root in many, many other places.

BETTING ON CULTURE CHANGE

On a Sunday morning in January 2016, a police officer named Doug Barney was murdered in Salt Lake City, Utah. Cory Lee Henderson was identified as the culprit and subsequently shot and killed by local police.

The details of the incident were almost guaranteed to provoke outrage. Barney was the father of three teenage daughters. A survivor of bladder cancer, he had volunteered to work overtime that weekend to help pay for his medical treatments. He died from a gunshot wound to the head.

By contrast, Henderson had an extensive criminal history, including serving both state and federal prison time for multiple drug and firearm offenses. At the time of Barney's murder, Henderson had absconded from a drug treatment facility where he had been sent by the parole board.

The reaction was immediate and intense. "We were receiving media attacks like I've never seen in my lifetime," remembers Rollin Cook, executive director of the Utah Department of Corrections.[22]

In the eyes of some critics, the tragedy was linked to a recent set of reforms, signed into law by Governor Gary Herbert, that sought to reduce the use of incarceration in the state. A local newspaper headline posed the question this way: "Did New Program Allow Man Who Killed Officer out of Prison Early?"[23]

Though its rate of imprisonment is well below the national average, Utah's prison population increased by 18 percent between 2004 and 2014.[24] Almost half of the prison population was made up of offenders revoked from parole or probation supervision,[25] and 63 percent of prison admissions in 2014 were for nonviolent offenses.[26] Excluding probation or parole revocation, simple drug possession was the number one reason for admission in 2013.[27]

In 2015, Utah governor Gary Herbert signed into law a package of sentencing and corrections reforms that are expected to eliminate almost all projected prison growth over the next twenty years, saving more than $500 million in the process.[28] Among other things, the legislation reduces the penalty for a first or second conviction of possession of a controlled substance to a misdemeanor; Utah is the first Republican-governed state to make possession of a drug other than marijuana a misdemeanor.[29] The legislation also establishes a standardized system that allows inmates to earn time off of their sentences for participating in programs designed to reduce recidivism upon release from prison.

While it is too soon to evaluate the long-term impact of Utah's package of criminal justice reforms in quantitative terms, it is notable that the death of police officer Doug Barney did not derail the initiative.

This resilience is almost entirely due to the strong showing of support—and what might be called a measure of decisive indecision—from local elected officials in the tragedy's immediate aftermath. According to Ron Gordon of the Utah Commission on Criminal and Juvenile Justice, local officials resisted overwhelming pressure to jettison the new legislation: "The governor, the speaker of the House, and the president of the Senate all said, 'We will wait to pass any judgment because it is too early to draw any conclusions.' That was very helpful. If those elected leaders had delivered a different message, we could be in a very different position right now."[30]

This is not typically how these things play out, at least not in the United States over the past generation. Reformers live in understandable fear of bad cases. There's good reason for this: recent history is littered with examples of states moving quickly in the wake of tragedy to enact a strong "tough on crime" legislative response. A lot of eponymous law gets made this way—Megan's Law, Kendra's Law, and so on. Without addressing the merits of these particular pieces of legislation, legal wisdom has long held that hard cases make bad law. In other words, the immediate aftermath of a unique tragedy may not be the best time to construct new frameworks that will govern how thousands of future cases will be handled.

Having resisted this temptation, reformers in Utah are now turning their attention to a very different kind of obstacle: making sure the changes authorized by law actually make a difference on the ground. As difficult as it is to pass bipartisan legislation in an era of political polarization, ensuring good implementation within government agencies may be more difficult. Gordon has become a realist about the challenges of implementation:

> When you're working on statewide implementation, you'd like to see entire agencies change [quickly]. That's not really the way it ever happens with culture change. Individual people within the agency change, and slowly start bringing along others. We might have a few years ago thought that we could make a round of presentations and respond to questions and then be well on our way. We were a little bit foolish because this requires an ongoing intensive effort.

Reformers in Utah are working hard to ensure that a high-profile tragedy will not undermine years of painstaking research, planning, and negotiation. They have good reason to be concerned: that's exactly what happened in Arkansas.

"Arkansas in 2011 passes a hugely ambitious justice reform bill that results in an abrupt decline of their prison population," Zoë Towns says. "Then two and a half years later, a parolee commits a terrible crime."[31] Towns is talking about Darrel Dennis. In 2008, Darrel Dennis was released on parole after serving time for aggravated robbery. Over the next four and a half years, Dennis was arrested over two dozen times (including multiple felony charges). But his parole was never revoked, and in May 2013 he was released from Pulaski County Jail, where he was being held for a technical violation. Two days later he shot and killed eighteen-year-old Forest Abrams.[32] After this incident, the parole board shut the door. Arkansas now has the second-fastest rate of prison population growth in the country. And this rapid growth is a direct response to a single crime.

Management theorist Peter Drucker is credited with coining the expression "Culture eats strategy for breakfast."[33] In declaring that the underlying values of an institution trump even the most clever plans, Drucker was primarily concerned with promoting deeper understanding of organizational dynamics within corporations, but the same observation applies to the justice system.

Cultural change should be the ultimate goal of criminal justice reform. At its root, this means seeing the fundamental humanity in all defendants, regardless of their race or gender or socioeconomic status—and treating them accordingly. Translating this ideal into practice can be a challenge.

In a recent report cataloging the results of the Justice Reinvestment Initiative, the Urban Institute affirms this reality:

> One of the greatest challenges for states is translating reform legislation into reality. New policies often require multiple agencies to change how they do business, and resistance is common. Educating stakeholders about reforms, securing buy-in, and changing daily practices takes time, and enthusiasm for reform can wane. States must also grapple with changes in the political climate (e.g., staff turnover or loss of administrative or legislative champions), pushback from key players such as judges or district attorneys, and aggressive efforts to undo reform provisions.[34]

Utah is not out of the woods yet, but reformers are making some headway. "I've been doing corrections for coming up on twenty-eight years," says Rollin Cook of the Utah Department of Corrections, "and this is really the first time that you've seen both sides of the aisle starting to talk about these folks as people, and that for us to make a change with them, we can't treat them like animals. You've got to treat them with respect. Provide them opportunities. Provide them the tools—things that help them succeed."[35]

As Cook indicates, state-level reformers have been aided by changing attitudes toward drug use. Addiction used to be viewed primarily as a moral failure. Today, after years of advocacy by public health reformers, we have a more nuanced understanding of addiction as a disease.[36]

★   ★   ★

Experience teaches us that reforming the justice system is both art and science—be it in Utah, Georgia, Mississippi, or New York City.[37]

If we are to do this right, we need to be nerds. We need to be clear thinkers who look at data and consult the latest social science and statistical techniques. But we also need to be guided by compassion and remember that the justice system is not an abstract process or a series of numbers on a page. It is a collection of people. And no matter what role they have been assigned in this drama—be they police officers or perpetrators, concerned citizens or community corrections officials—all of these actors are animated by the same tangle of motivations and idiosyncrasies that always drive human behavior. We can never hope to improve justice unless we wrestle with this reality.

Seizing the current window of opportunity means more than just identifying the right policy goals or providing money to scale up model programs. We need to be thoughtful about the details of implementation, and give practitioners the tools and training they need to do things differently. We need to actively engage frontline justice professionals in the reform process to ensure that they will take ownership of new ideas rather than working behind the scenes to subvert them.

This process is under way in places like Utah, Georgia, and Mississippi. Even Arkansas has returned to the challenge of criminal justice reform in an effort to tackle the new growth spurred by the changes to parole post–Darrel Dennis. We need to make sure that other places follow suit. And we must also have the patience and resolve to pursue the goals of reform not just for an election cycle or two, but over the course of a decade or more. There are no quick fixes or easy solutions here. But there is a lot of room for improvement.

CONCLUSION:
A WHOLE BUNCH OF LIGHTBULBS

John Tharp was only two weeks into his job as the sheriff of Lucas County, Ohio, in January 2013 when he met with the Board of County Commissioners to request a new jail facility. A decorated veteran of the Vietnam War, Tharp had spent over half of his forty-four years in law enforcement with the Toledo Police Department. He knew full well that the Lucas County jail had been under a federal court order to address overcrowded conditions since the day it opened in the late 1970s. "Everybody knew it, but we didn't have a lot of people wanting to talk about it," recalls Tharp.[1] He decided he was going to change all of that.

"It's a cesspool," says Tharp of the jail, which was built to house just under 350 inmates at a time, but which regularly operates at over 120 percent of its capacity. The local newspaper describes "sardine-like conditions" inside the jail: "Holding cells are stuffed beyond the recommended capacity and other rooms in the facility have been converted into holding cells just to accommodate demand."[2] According to Tharp, "The roofs are leaking, the pipes are breaking, and the elevator's breaking down. I am no expert, but common sense will tell you that it's not humane for the inmates, it's not humane for the employees."

Along with overcrowding, the jail in Lucas County has another problem: nearly six out of ten inmates are African American in a county that is only 20 percent black.[3]

Sheriff Tharp knew that the county commissioners might be skeptical about building a new jail, but even he was surprised by the response when they were presented with estimates of how the jail population was expected to grow. For the commissioners, it wasn't just a lightbulb moment—"that was more like an explosion of a whole bunch of lightbulbs," recalls Lucas County Commissioner Carol Contrada.[4]

"I can remember handing the projections to Commissioner Contrada," recollects Matthew Heyrman, the director of Public Health and Safety for the Board of County Commissioners. "She just had this look on her face like, 'You've *got* to be kidding me.'"[5] According to Contrada: "Even if we made certain changes [to reduce the use of jail], we would still need a bed capacity of 620, almost double the size of the jail that we have now. It was like, 'You mean we have to build a jail twice as big, even if we *do* make changes?' It was just appalling to us that that would be."

Led by Commissioner Contrada and Sheriff Tharp, Lucas County decided to hit the pause button. Rather than building a new jail, they decided to ask a different set of questions: Who is in jail? How did they get there? And might there be a better way—more effective, humane, and affordable—to respond to criminal behavior?

The questions that Lucas County began to wrestle with back in 2013 (and continues to wrestle with today) are the same questions that have animated our work. In writing this book, we have tried to tell the stories of committed reformers on the front lines of criminal justice—judges and academics and social workers and community activists and politicians who are laboring each and every day to reduce incarceration, improve neighborhood safety, and make our justice system as fair as it can be. Many of these people are our friends and colleagues, people we have worked alongside at the Center for Court Innovation as they have tried to test new approaches to doing justice.

In telling their stories, we have attempted to make the case that reforming our justice system is both harder and easier than it looks. In recent years, calls for fundamental change have reverberated across the United States. The #cut50 movement, led by celebrity advocate Van Jones, is just one example of the efforts to roll back incarceration that are currently under way. To achieve their stated goal—cutting our incarceration rate in half—will be difficult. Of course, reducing incarceration is not the only goal worth pursuing. When you add in trying to transform crime-plagued neighborhoods or promote public trust in justice or change the behavior of individuals who return to the justice system over and over again, the degree of difficulty just escalates further.

Setting ambitious goals is an important part of the reform process. But even as we move toward these goals, we must acknowledge the obstacles to fundamental change, be they political, cultural, logistical, or financial. And we must set realistic expectations. If we fail to do so, we run the risk of engendering disappointment and deepening public cynicism about government. So these pages contain no silver bullet solutions. Instead, we have written about the realities of reform on the ground, which often has a two-steps-forward, one-step-back dynamic.

While we do not offer the thrill of a simple rallying cry, we have attempted to spell out real-life, actionable changes in the day-to-day operations of the justice system that might meaningfully (and safely) reduce the use of jail and prison. And here is the positive part of our message. We believe it is not necessary to solve the problems of poverty or racism or inequality (though these should be addressed, of course) in order to achieve significant change within the justice system. There are concrete steps that we can take in the here and now in order to improve justice in the United States. Broadly speaking, they fall into three categories.

First, we must orient our system to preventing crime rather than reacting to crime after it occurs. Crime prevention efforts need to be targeted to high-risk neighborhoods and high-risk individuals. They need to involve local residents in their design, implementation, and evaluation. And they need to be given plenty of time; we know from our own experience in places like Brownsville, Brooklyn, that investments in developing young people or changing the physical landscape of a community often take years to bear fruit.

Second, we must treat every defendant and every victim with dignity, respect, and empathy. We have seen repeatedly that today's victim is tomorrow's defendant—and vice versa. Trauma is pervasive within the justice system. Interventions that seek to change the behavior of offending populations must acknowledge this reality. Every defendant deserves to have their voice heard and to understand how the criminal justice process works. Too many people leave criminal court without any comprehension of what has just happened to them. As we have seen in places like Newark, New Jersey, and Red Hook, Brooklyn, changing the architecture of the justice system to make it more user-friendly and taking the time to communicate more clearly with defendants and victims alike will go a long way toward enhancing public trust in justice and promoting compliance with court orders.

Third, we must expand the array of sanctions available to judges and prosecutors so that they do not default to incarceration because it is the simplest, easiest option. These decision-makers need more options at every stage of the process; we should be building off-ramps at the point of arrest, during the pretrial period, and at sentencing.

We believe that there should be consequences for criminal behavior. But, except in fairly rare circumstances, these consequences need not be incarceration. In these pages, we have attempted to shine a spotlight on alternatives to incarceration that are meaningful and effective. These include programs that work with both low-level offenders and those that have committed serious felony offenses. One thing that many of these efforts share is a commitment to the latest social science research, which suggests that the system must carefully assess the risks and needs presented by individual defendants and use this information to match them to appropriate interventions.

As we write this, our country is entering uncharted waters. Will Donald Trump halt the momentum that criminal justice reformers have worked so hard to create? Will the political polarization that characterized the election of 2016 make it harder to build consensus for change going forward?

We cannot predict the answers to these questions. But we have tried to articulate an approach to criminal justice reform that we think will appeal across a broad political spectrum, including both Republicans and Democrats. We have also highlighted a fundamental truth about criminal justice reform: as important as the president and Congress can be in terms of setting the terms of public debate, at the end of the day most of the action is at the state and local level. And there is plenty of progress to report in numerous states and cities across the country, including Lucas County, Ohio.

In pursuing change, John Tharp and his compatriots in Lucas County have touched on many of the elements that we have described in these pages. For example, in 2015, Lucas County implemented a risk assessment tool with an eye toward reducing the use of pretrial detention. The *New York Times* credited these efforts with both increasing the number of defendants released without bail and decreasing the number of defendants arrested while out on bail.[6]

Building on this foundation, Lucas County was selected to participate in the MacArthur Foundation's Safety and Justice Challenge, a national jail-reduction competition that drew 191 applicants across forty-five states.[7] In addition to planning meetings with the criminal justice practitioners, the Lucas County stakeholders engaged local residents in the process, with a focus on reducing racial and ethnic disparities.[8] Along the way, Lucas County has also managed to train all of its judges in procedural justice principles.

All of these positive steps were threatened when the City of Toledo, which comprises 64 percent of Lucas County, stopped paying the bill for its sentenced jail population. Toledo had been paying for beds in the Lucas County jail going back to the 1970s, but a long-pending lawsuit to discontinue these payments had suddenly been decided in its favor. "I remember thinking this is going to be a day from hell," recalls Matthew Heyrman, of the Lucas County Board of Commissioners. "I knew at that moment the county would be out of millions and millions of dollars."[9]

Lucas County has separate facilities for the sentenced population and the pretrial population. "We could not allow [the sentenced] facility to close," says Commissioner Carol Contrada. "It would have been a public safety crisis."[10] To fend off calamity, Lucas County decided it needed to find a way to reduce the sentenced jail population by 30 percent. "We didn't have the money, so we reduced the beds," explains Contrada.

Lucas County essentially limited the number of beds each judge could utilize at any one time. They sold this initially unpopular idea to local judges by offering them new ways to deal with sentenced defendants. For starters, judges would be given increased access to community-based alternatives like electronic monitoring. They would also be given the ability to review the risks and needs of the jail population in real time. Each judge in Lucas County would be able to see the risk and need profiles of their entire portfolio, including those individuals who had already been sentenced to jail. The idea here was to help judges make more nuanced decisions about who should be in and who should be out based on the availability of jail beds and the threat to public safety presented by each defendant.

After some handwringing, the judges agreed to give the new approach a try. Contrada and Heyrman held their breath.

It worked. Judges started moving individuals out of the jail and resentencing them to community-based alternatives. The numbers began to drop, and all of a sudden 30 percent felt well within reach. But Contrada and Heyrman were in no way expecting what would come next. "The number just kept dropping," exclaims Heyrman. "The judges are getting no pressure to continue dropping the number beyond the 30 percent target yet they continue to do it."

In other words, when judges in Lucas County were given better information and the right resources, they changed their practice and significantly reduced the use of incarceration. Good sense prevailed.

It is too soon to declare victory in Lucas County. But it is not too soon to take away some early lessons—and a message of hope for the future. Lucas County has shown that a series of seemingly modest, commonsense improvements—using risk and need assessments, training criminal justice professionals in procedural justice, expanding community-based alternatives to incarceration, and engaging local residents in the process—can add up to significant change. In so doing, Lucas County offers a preliminary blueprint for reformers searching for how to reduce incarceration and improve the justice system. Lucas County had its lightbulb moment. Now we need to figure out how to make a whole bunch of lightbulbs go off across the United States.

ACKNOWLEDGMENTS

First, all praise is due Diane Wachtell and The New Press. The basic idea for this book came out of a conversation with Diane in 2015. We are grateful for the existence of an editor with an interest in criminal justice and a publisher with a commitment to books about public policy.

Second, this book would not be possible were it not for the Center for Court Innovation, the agency where we both work. The Center provided us with time and space to write. More important, it provided us with inspiration. This book chronicles many of the reform efforts and ideas that the Center for Court Innovation has championed over the years. We hope we have done them justice in these pages.

We thank the people who helped give birth to the Center for Court Innovation in the early 1990s, among them John Feinblatt (the Center's founding director), Mary McCormick, Eric Lee, Michele Sviridoff, the late Judith S. Kaye, and Jonathan Lippman. We also thank the policymakers and funders who support the Center on an ongoing basis. This includes the New York court system (Janet DiFiore, Larry Marks, and Ron Younkins), the New York City Mayor's Office (Liz

Glazer), the Bureau of Justice Assistance, and the John D. and Catherine T. MacArthur Foundation (Laurie Garduque, Soledad McGrath, Patrick Griffin, and Maurice Classen), among others.

Dozens of our friends and colleagues at the Center for Court Innovation contributed to this book, offering advice and feedback and encouragement. We thank Adam Mansky, Liberty Aldrich, Michael Rempel, Sarah Fritsche, Julius Lang, Rob Wolf, Courtney Bryan, Katie Crank, Erika Sasson, Kate Barrow, Yolaine Menyard, and Jennifer Tallon for their help.

More specifically, we thank Samiha Amin Meah for her help with infographics. We thank Serin Choi, Phil Bowen, and Matthew Watkins for their comments on the introduction. We thank Raphael Pope-Sussman for his contributions to chapter 1. We thank James Brodick, Erica Tapia, Deron Johnston, Amy Ellenbogen, Kenton Kirby, and Ife Charles for helping us with chapter 2. We thank Jethro Antoine, Kelly Mulligan-Brown, Emily LaGratta, Victoria Pratt, Alex Calabrese, and Amanda Berman for their assistance with chapter 3. We thank Aisha Greene and Lenore Lebron for their help with chapter 5. We thank Aaron Arnold and Valerie Raine for their comments on chapter 6. Rebecca Thomforde-Hauser helped us with chapter 7. And we could not have pushed this book over the finish line without the help of Isabella Banks, Rebecca Thomson, Tamar Hoffman, Patrick McMenamin, and Lauren Speigel, who provided research support and spent hours cleaning up the manuscript.

Beyond the Center for Court Innovation, our thanks to everyone who agreed to be interviewed for this book. Some of these people are our friends. Some are people we met for the first time through this process. What they all have in common is a passion for improving the criminal justice system. We thank them for sharing their time and ideas with us.

Finally, we offer the following personal thanks.

Greg: To Carolyn, Hannah, and Milly Berman—it is a blessing to live with three great writers and funny people. Thanks for bringing mirth and kindness and perspective to my life. To Michele and Allan Berman—thanks for believing in my potential. And to M.J.—thanks for modeling perseverance and grace in the face of adversity.

Julian: To Erica Adler—for endless love and unflinching support. To Amelia and August "Auggie" Adler—for so much inspiration, so much warmth, so much tomfoolery. And to Helen and Elliot Adler—for keeping the faith.

NOTES

Introduction

1. Jed S. Rakoff, "Mass Incarceration: The Silence of the Judges," *New York Review of Books*, May 21, 2015, accessed January 20, 2017, http://www.nybooks.com/articles/2015/05/21/mass-incarceration -silence-judges.
2. Jim Manzi, "What Social Science Does—and Doesn't—Know," *City Journal*, Summer 2010, accessed February 10, 2017, https://www .city-journal.org/html/what-social-science-does%E2%80%94and -doesn%E2%80%99t%E2%80%94know-13297.html.
3. James Forman Jr., "Racial Critiques of Mass Incarceration: Beyond the New Jim Crow," *Racial Critiques* 87 (2012): 125.
4. James Forman Jr., *Locking Up Our Own* (New York: Farrar, Straus and Giroux, 2017), 229.
5. German Lopez, "Want to End Mass Incarceration? This Poll Should Worry You," *Vox*, September 7, 2016, accessed January 20, 2017, http://www.vox.com/2016/9/7/12814504/mass-incarceration-poll.
6. Adam Gopnik, "Naked Cities: The Death and Life of Urban America," *The New Yorker*, October 5, 2015, accessed June 9, 2016, http:// www.newyorker.com/magazine/2015/10/05/naked cities.

1. Who Is Behind Bars?

1. *Correctional Populations in the United States, 2014*, Bureau of Justice Statistics; Prisoners in 2014, Bureau of Justice Statistics.
2. Michael Schwirtz and Michael Winerip, "Violence by Rikers Guards Grew Under Bloomberg," *New York Times*, August 14, 2014, accessed January 20, 2017, https://www.nytimes.com/2014/08/14 /nyregion/why-violence-toward-inmates-at-rikers-grew.html.

3. Michael Jacobson, "Propelling Multi-sector Social Innovation to Advance Smart Decarceration" (presentation, Smart Decarceration Initiative's Inaugural Conference: "From Mass Incarceration to Effective and Sustainable Decarceration," St. Louis, MO, September 24–27, 2015).

4. "World Prison Brief: Prison Population Total," Institute for Criminal Policy Research, accessed September 7, 2016, http://www.prisonstudies.org/highest-to-lowest/prison-population-total?field_region_taxonomy_tid=All. Technically, the tiny island nation of Seychelles (population 90,000) has the distinction of most incarcerated per capita. The country's prison population rate per 100,000 of national population in 2014 was 799. We're second. See "World Prison Brief: Seychelles," Institute for Criminal Policy Research, accessed September 7, 2016, http://www.prisonstudies.org/country/seychelles.

5. Danielle Kaeble, Lauren Glaze, Anastasious Tsoutis, and Todd Minton, "Correctional Populations in the United States, 2014," Bureau of Justice Statistics, 4, accessed May 24, 2017, https://www.bjs.gov/content/pub/pdf/cpus14.pdf. This represents all individuals eighteen and over in state and federal prisons and local jails. Note that it does not include youth under eighteen who have been tried and sentenced as adults.

6. According to the Bureau of Justice Statistics, "incarceration rate" refers to the total number of inmates in local, state, or federal custody per 100,000 individuals. "Imprisonment rate" is also sometimes used for measuring the scope of incarceration, but that only accounts for the number of individuals sentenced for over one year and excludes all pretrial inmates and local jail inmates. See Kaeble et al., "Correctional Populations in the United States, 2014," 10.

7. Calculation based on data from Kaeble et al., "Correctional Populations in the United States, 2014," and "World Prison Brief: United Kingdom: England & Wales," Institute for Criminal Policy

Research, accessed September 7, 2016, http://www.prisonstudies
.org/country/united-kingdom-england-wales.

8. Calculation based on data from Kaeble et al., "Correctional Populations in the United States, 2014," and "World Prison Brief: Norway,"
Institute for Criminal Policy Research, accessed September 7, 2016,
http://www.prisonstudies.org/country/norway.

9. That said, the female jail population is growing rapidly.

10. E. Ann Carson, "Prisoners in 2014," Bureau of Justice Statistics, 15,
accessed September 7, 2016, https://www.bjs.gov/content/pub/pdf
/p14.pdf; "QuickFacts: Race and Hispanic Origin," United States
Census Bureau, accessed September 7, 2016, http://www.census.gov
/quickfacts/table/RHI725215/00.

11. "Estimated number of persons supervised by U.S. adult correctional
systems, by correctional status, 1980–2014," Bureau of Justice Statistics, last modified July 19, 2016, http://www.bjs.gov/content/key
statistics/excel/Correctional_population_counts_by_status_1980
-2014.xlsx.

12. Kaeble et al., "Correctional Populations in the United States, 2014,"
2; Carson, "Prisoners in 2014," 16–17. There are also approximately
seventy thousand juveniles serving mandates in residential placement,
primarily for delinquency. They are not considered "incarcerated"
and as such are not generally counted in tallies of the incarcerated
population. See Melissa Sickmund and Charles Puzzanchera, "Juvenile Offenders and Victims: 2014 National Report," *National Center
for Juvenile Justice* (2014): 187, accessed January 17, 2017, http://www
.ojjdp.gov/ojstatbb/nr2014/downloads/NR2014.pdf.

13. Calculation based on data from Todd D. Minton and Zhen Zeng,
"Jail Inmates at Midyear 2014," Bureau of Justice Statistics, 7, accessed January 17, 2017, http://www.bjs.gov/content/pub/pdf
/jim14.pdf; Carson, "Prisoners in 2014," 10.

14. "World Prison Brief: Prison Population Total," Institute for Criminal
Policy Research, accessed May 24, 2017, http://www.prisonstudies

.org/highest-to-lowest/prison-population-total. Again, technically, just below the Seychelles in per capita imprisonment.

15. James Forman Jr., *Locking Up Our Own: Crime and Punishment in Black America* (New York: Farrar, Straus and Giroux, 2017), 148.

16. Jeremy Travis (president, John Jay College of Criminal Justice), interview with author, January 13, 2016. Unless otherwise indicated, all subsequent quotations are taken from this interview.

17. For example, see Dana Goldstein, "How to Cut the Prison Population by 50 Percent," *The Marshall Project*, March 4, 2015, accessed May 24, 2017, https://www.themarshallproject.org/2015/03/04/how-to-cut-the-prison-population-by-50-percent.

18. Kathleen Miles, "Just How Much the War on Drugs Impacts Our Overcrowded Prisons, in One Chart," *Huffington Post*, March 10, 2014, accessed January 17, 2017, http://www.huffingtonpost.com/2014/03/10/war-on-drugs-prisons-infographic_n_4914884.html.

19. "Fact Sheet: Trends in U.S. Corrections," The Sentencing Project, 2015, 2, accessed January 17, 2017, http://sentencingproject.org/wp-content/uploads/2016/01/Trends-in-US-Corrections.pdf.

20. Calculation based on data from Carson, "Prisoners in 2014," 30; Kaeble et al., "Correctional Populations in the United States, 2014."

21. Carson, "Prisoners in 2014," 16.

22. Leon Neyfakh, "Why Are So Many Americans in Prison?," *Slate*, February 6, 2015, accessed May 24, 2017, http://www.slate.com/articles/news_and_politics/crime/2015/02/mass_incarceration_a_provocative_new_theory_for_why_so_many_americans_are.html.

23. The U.S. Department of Justice defines simple assault as follows: "Attack without a weapon resulting either in no injury, minor injury (for example, bruises, black eyes, cuts, scratches or swelling) or in undetermined injury requiring less than 2 days of hospitalization. Also includes attempted assault without a weapon." See "Assault," Bureau of Justice Statistics, last modified February 17, 2016, accessed May 24, 2017, http://www.bjs.gov/index.cfm?ty=tp&tid=316.

24. "Robbery," Bureau of Justice Statistics, last modified February 11, 2016, accessed May 24, 2017, http://www.bjs.gov/index.cfm?ty=tp &tid=313.

25. Kevin E. McCarthy, "Office of Legislative Research Report: Felony Murder," Connecticut General Assembly, last modified February 13, 2008, accessed May 24, 2017, https://www.cga.ct.gov/2008 /rpt/2008-r-0087.htm. For the federal definition, see 18 U.S.C. § 1111(a).

26. While the circumstances under which the felony murder rule applies varies by state, this is certainly true in the more expansive felony murder rule provisions, such as that of Florida (Florida Statutes § 782.04 (1) (a)).

27. Adam Liptak, "Serving Life for Providing Car to Killers," *New York Times*, December 4, 2007, accessed January 17, 2017, http://www .nytimes.com/2007/12/04/us/04felony.html.

28. Carson, "Prisoners in 2014," 30.

29. Joseph A. Califano, "Substance Abuse and America's Prison Population 2010," National Center on Addiction and Substance Abuse at Columbia University, 2010, 10, accessed January 17, 2017, http:// www.centeronaddiction.org/addiction-research/reports/substance -abuse-prison-system-2010.

30. Substance use disorder rates are 65.2 percent in state prison, 65.8 percent in local jail, and 54.8 percent in federal prison. Califano, "Substance Abuse and America's Prison Population 2010," 25.

31. Doris J. James and Lauren E. Glaze, "Mental Health Problems of Prison and Jail Inmates," Bureau of Justice Statistics, 2006, 1, accessed January 17, 2017, http://www.bjs.gov/content/pub/pdf /mhppji.pdf. Note that this is the most recent BJS report concerning mental health although it was published ten years ago.

32. Overall, childhood abuse was reported by 14.4 percent of men and 36.7 percent of women, compared to general population rate estimates of 5 to 8 percent of men and 12 to 17 percent of women. See

Caroline Wolf Harlow, "Prior Abuse Reported by Inmates and Pro-bationers," Bureau of Justice Statistics, 1999, 2, accessed January 17, 2017, http://www.bjs.gov/content/pub/pdf/parip.pdf.

33. Ibid.

34. Aleks Kajstura and Russ Immarigeon, "States of Women's Incarceration: The Global Context," Prison Policy Initiative, accessed July 27, 2017, https://www.prisonpolicy.org/global/women.

35. Ibid.

36. Shannon M. Lynch et al., "Women's Pathways to Jail: The Roles and Intersections of Serious Mental Illness and Trauma," Bureau of Justice Statistics, 2012, 14, accessed January 17, 2017, https://www.bja .gov/Publications/Women_Pathways_to_Jail.pdf.

37. Irina Alexandrovna Komarovskaya et al., "Exploring Gender Differences in Trauma Exposure and the Emergence of Symptoms of PTSD Among Incarcerated Men and Women," *Journal of Forensic Psychiatry & Psychology* 22 (2011): 395–410, accessed January 17, 2017, doi: 10.1080/14789949.2011.572989. This study used the DSM-IV-TR standards for PTSD. Combat-related PTSD afflicts between 4 and 17 percent of U.S. Iraq War veterans. See Lisa K. Richardson, B. Christopher Frueh, and Ronald Acierno, "Prevalence Estimates of Combat-Related PTSD: A Critical Review," *Australian and New Zealand Journal of Psychiatry* 44 (2010): 4–19, accessed January 17, 2017, doi: 10.3109/00048670903393597.

38. Jamiles Lartey, "Women in Jails Are the Fastest Growing Incarcerated Population, Study Says," *The Guardian*, August 17, 2016, accessed July 31, 2017, https://www.theguardian.com/us-news/2016 /aug/17/women-incarceration-rates-growth-study.

39. Michael Garcia Bochenek, "Children Behind Bars: The Global Overuse of Detention of Children," Human Rights Watch, accessed July 27, 2017, https://www.hrw.org/world-report/2016 /children-behind-bars.

40. Gary Gately, "Should Young Adult Offenders Be Treated More Like Juveniles?," *Juvenile Justice Information Exchange*, June 5, 2014,

accessed May 25, 2017, http://jjie.org/2014/06/05/should-young
-adult-offenders-be-treated-more-like-juveniles.

41. "Old Behind Bars: The Aging Prison Population in the United
States," Human Rights Watch, last modified January 27, 2012,
https://www.hrw.org/report/2012/01/27/old-behind-bars/aging
-prison-population-united-states.

42. Ilan H. Meyer et al., "Incarceration Rates and Traits of Sexual Mi-
norities in the United States: National Inmate Survey, 2011–2012,"
AJLH Transgender Health 107 (2017): 234–240, accessed July 27, 2017,
doi: 10.2105/AJPH.2016.303576.

43. Tom Caiazza, "Release: Broken Criminal Justice System Dispropor-
tionately Targets and Harms LGBT People," Center for American
Progress, February 23, 2016, accessed July 30, 2017, https://www
.americanprogress.org/press/release/2016/02/23/131547/release
-broken-criminal-justice-system-disproportionately-targets-and
-harms-lgbt-people.

44. Determining the precise recidivism rates of inmates with mental
illness is methodologically challenging given data collection con-
straints, but having a serious mental illness does correlate with a
higher rate of re-offending. See Jacques Baillargeon, Stephen K.
Hoge, and Joseph V. Penn, "Addressing the Challenge of Community Reentry Among Released Inmates with Serious Mental Illness,"
American Journal of Community Psychology 46 (2010): 361–75, accessed
January 17, 2017, doi: 10.1007/s10464-010-9345-6.

45. Alex Calabrese (presiding judge, Red Hook Community Justice
Center), correspondence with author, February 22, 2016.

46. Faye Taxman (criminologist, George Mason University), interview
with author, August 3, 2015.

2. Planting Seeds

1. *The Character of Police Work: Strategic and Tactical Implications*, Center
for Applied Social Research, Northeastern University (2016).

2. This chapter borrows some language from a white paper by Greg Berman entitled "Advancing Community Justice: The Challenge of Brownsville, Brooklyn," published by the Center for Court Innovation in 2015 and available at: http://www.courtinnovation.org/sites /default/files/documents/Advancing_Community_Justice.pdf.

3. "The Brownsville Partnership," Community Solutions, 2016, accessed January 23, 2017, https://cmtysolutions.org/brownsvillepart nership.

4. "Crime and Safety Report Rankings: Safest for Violent Crimes," DNA Info, accessed January 23, 2017, http://www.dnainfo.com /new-york/crime-safety-report/ranking#violent. Since the time this was initially written, Brownsville's ranking has changed to second-to-last.

5. Camille Bautista, "Youth Clubhouse Opens in Brownsville Lot to Provide Safe Community Space," *DNA Info*, October 18, 2016, accessed January 23, 2016, https://www.dnainfo.com/new -york/20161018/brownsville/brownsville-youth-community-club house-shipping-containers.

6. Viola Greene-Walker (district manager, Community Board #16, Brooklyn, New York), interview with author, November 7, 2016. Unless indicated otherwise, all subsequent quotations are taken from this interview.

7. Suvi Hynynen, "Community Perceptions of Brownsville: A Survey of Neighborhood Quality of Life, Safety, and Services," *Center for Court Innovation* (2011): 3, accessed January 23, 2017, http:// www.courtinnovation.org/sites/default/files/documents/Browns ville%20Op%20Data%20FINAL.pdf.

8. Bautista, "Youth Clubhouse Opens in Brownsville Lot to Provide Safe Community Space."

9. Natasha Haverty, "What if 10 Percent of Your Neighbors Went to Prison Downstate?," North County Public Radio, April 1, 2014, accessed January 23, 2017, http://www.northcountrypublicradio.org

/news/story/24479/20140401/what-if-10-percent-of-your-neigh
bors-went-to-prison-downstate.

10. Benjamin Weiser and Joseph Goldstein, "Mayor Says New York
City Will Settle Suits on Stop-and-Frisk Tactics," *New York Times,*
January 30, 2014, accessed January 23, 2017, http://www.ny
times.com/2014/01/31/nyregion/de-blasio-stop-and-frisk.html
?hpw&rref=nyregion.

11. Sarah Picard-Fritsche, Rachel Swaner, and Suvi Hynynen Lambson, "Deterrence and Legitimacy in Brownsville, Brooklyn: A Process Evaluation of the Brownsville Anti-Violence Project," *Center
for Court Innovation* (2014): accessed January 23, 2017, http://www
.courtinnovation.org/sites/default/files/documents/BAVP_Report
.pdf.

12. Xavier Pittman (Brownsville resident), interview with author, October 11, 2016.

13. Tshaka Barrows (deputy director, W. Haywood Burns Institute),
interview with author, June 2, 2016.

14. Mark Soler (executive director, Children's Center for Law and Policy), interview with author, June 16, 2016.

15. James Brodick (director, Brownsville Community Justice Center),
interview with author, October 11, 2016. Unless otherwise indicated, all subsequent quotations are taken from this interview.

16. Donna Coker (law professor, University of Miami), interview with
author, June 16, 2016. Unless otherwise indicated, all subsequent
quotations are taken from this interview.

17. "Creating a Trauma-Informed Criminal Justice System for Women:
Why and How," Substance Abuse and Mental Health Services
Administration, 2013, 1, accessed January 27, 2017, http://www
.nasmhpd.org/sites/default/files/Women%20in%20Corrections
%20TIC%20SR(2).pdf.

18. Julian Adler, Sarah Picard-Fritsche, Suvi Hynynen Lambson, War-
ren Reich, and Michael Rempel, "Predictors of Re-Arrest in the

Misdemeanor Population in New York City," unpublished raw data, *Center for Court Innovation* (2014).

19. Victoria Dexter (vice president of mental health treatment, Safe Horizon Counseling Center), interview with author, April, 5, 2016. Unless otherwise indicated, all subsequent quotations are taken from this interview.

20. Lenore Anderson (founder and executive director, Californians for Safety and Justice), interview with author, June 3, 2016.

21. Kenton Kirby (program coordinator, Make It Happen), correspondence with author, June 15, 2016.

22. Amy Ellenbogen (director, Crown Heights Community Mediation Center), interview with author, January 20, 2017.

23. Sharon "Ife" Charles (citywide anti-violence coordinator, Center for Court Innovation), interview with author, December 28, 2016.

24. Samuel Lieberman, "'Make It Happen' Program Offers Outlet for Youths Haunted by Memories of Violence," Juvenile Justice Information Exchange, March 4, 2015, accessed January 23, 2017, http://jjie.org/2015/03/04/make-it-happen-program-offers-outlet-for-youths-haunted-by-memories-of-violence.

25. Kenton Kirby (program coordinator, Make It Happen), interview with author, May 27, 2016.

26. Lieberman, "'Make It Happen' Program Offers Outlet for Youths Haunted by Memories of Violence."

27. Kenton Kirby, "'Guilty Victims' Have Suffered Too and Deserve Our Care," Think Justice Blog/Beyond Innocence, September 13, 2015, accessed January 23, 2017, https://www.vera.org/blog/beyond-innocence/guilty-victims-have-suffered-too-and-deserve-our-care-1.

28. Charlotte Gill, "Community Interventions," in David Weisburd, David P. Farrington, and Charlotte Gill (eds.), *What Works in Crime Prevention and Rehabilitation: Lessons from Systematic Reviews* (New York: Springer, 2016), 77–109.

29. Ibid., 98.

30. Erica Mateo (director of community-based initiatives, Brownsville Community Justice Center), interview with author, November 7, 2016. Unless otherwise indicated, all subsequent quotations are taken from this interview.

31. Rikki Reyna and Erin Durkin, "Brownsville Is Brooklyn's Worst Neighborhood for Children due to High Poverty, Lousy Access to Fresh Food and Day Care," *New York Daily News*, March 26, 2017, accessed May 24, 2017, http://www.nydailynews.com/new-york /brooklyn/brownsville-brooklyn-worst-neighborhood-children -article-1.3009978.

32. Jeffrey Fagan and G. Davies, "A Natural History of Neighborhood Violence," *Journal of Contemporary Criminal Justice* 20 (2004): 127–47; David S. Kirk and Andrew V. Papachristos "Cultural Mechanisms and the Persistence of Neighborhood Violence," *American Journal of Sociology* 116 (2011): 1190–1233.

33. Glenn Pierce, Susan Spaar, and LeBaron R. Briggs, *The Character of Police Work: Strategic and Tactical Implications* (Boston: Center for Applied Social Research, Northeastern University, 1988); David Weisburd, Shawn Bushway, Cynthia Lum, and Sue-Ming Yang, "Trajectories of Crime at Places: A Longitudinal Study of Street Segments in the City of Seattle," *Criminology* 42 (2004): 283–321.

34. Pierce, Spaar, and Briggs, *The Character of Police Work*.

35. Robert Bursik and Harold G. Grasmick, *Neighborhoods and Crime: The Dimensions of Effective Community Control* (New York: Lexington Books, 1993).

36. Devon Page (Brownsville resident), interview with author, January 19, 2017.

3. Taming the Green Monster

1. *Examining the Work of State Courts: An Overview of 2015 State Court Case Loads*, National Center for State Courts (2016).

2. Randy Burley (New Hope Baptist Church Soup Kitchen), interview with author, May 2, 2016. Unless otherwise indicated, all subsequent quotations are taken from this interview.

3. Felicia R. Osborne (senior pastor, Newark's Bethel Family and Youth Resource Center), interview with author, May 3, 2016.

4. "Investigation of the Newark Police Department," United States Department of Justice Civil Rights Division and United States Attorney's Office District of New Jersey, 2014, 47, accessed January 17, 2017, https://www.justice.gov/sites/default/files/crt/legacy/2014/07/22/newark_findings_7-22-14.pdf.

5. In 2015 the estimated population of Newark was 281,944. "QuickFacts: Newark, New Jersey," United States Census Bureau, accessed September 15, 2016, http://www.census.gov/quickfacts/table/PST045215/3451000; James Simpson (director, Newark Municipal Court), correspondence with author, May 4, 2016. In 2015, 42,529 criminal cases were added to the calendar of the Newark Municipal Court.

6. Ashlie Gibbons (assistant public defender, City of Newark), interview with author, April 13, 2016. Unless otherwise indicated, all subsequent quotations are taken from this interview.

7. "Community Justice in Newark: Needs Assessment and Implementation Recommendations," *Center for Court Innovation and the New Jersey Institute for Social Justice*, July 15, 2009, 19.

8. As we write this, it remains to be seen whether the justice department under Attorney General Jeff Sessions will continue this initiative.

9. "Justice Department Announces Resources to Assist State and Local Reform of Fine and Fee Practices," United States Department of Justice, last modified March 14, 2016, https://www.justice.gov/opa/pr/justice-department-announces-resources-assist-state-and-local-reform-fine-and-fee-practices.

10. Alexandra Natapoff (professor, Loyola Law School), interview with author, April 20, 2016. Unless otherwise indicated, all subsequent quotations are taken from this interview.

11. Newark Community Solutions is an operating project of the Center for Court Innovation.

12. Local Talk News Editor, "Mayor Booker and Newark Municipal Court Hold Opening Ceremony for Newark Community Solutions," *Local Talk News*, June 27, 2011.

13. Abram Brown, "Newark Introduces Court Program to Offer Community Service for Minor Offenses," *Star-Ledger*, June 17, 2011, accessed January 18, 2017, http://www.nj.com/news/index.ssf/2011/06/newark_officials_announce_new.html.

14. "Newark Community Solutions Annual Report: Year 2015," *Newark Community Solutions* (2015): 55–59.

15. Kerry Mulligan-Brown (project director, Newark Community Solutions), correspondence with author, May 5, 2016.

16. Tina Rosenberg, "The Simple Idea That Could Transform US Criminal Justice," *The Guardian*, June 23, 2015, accessed January 18, 2017, http://www.theguardian.com/us-news/2015/jun/23/procedural-justice-transform-us-criminal-courts.

17. Kerry Mulligan-Brown (project director, Newark Community Solutions), correspondence with author, April 20, 2016.

18. Ibid.

19. Alexandra Natapoff, "Misdemeanors," *Southern California Law Review* 85 (2012): 1313–75, accessed January 18, 2017, http://lawreview.usc.edu/issues/past/view/download/?id=1000559.

20. Ram Subramanian, Ruth Delaney, Stephen Roberts, Nancy Fishman, and Peggy McGarry, "Incarceration's Front Door: The Misuse of Jails in America," *Vera Institute for Justice* (2015): 5, accessed January 18, 2017, http://www.vera.org/sites/default/files/resources/downloads/incarcerations-front-door-report.pdf.

21. Stephanie Clifford and Joseph Goldstein, "Brooklyn Prosecutor Limits When He'll Target Marijuana," *New York Times*, July 8, 2014, accessed January 18, 2017, http://www.nytimes.com/2014/07/09/nyregion/brooklyn-district-attorney-to-stop-prosecuting-low-level-marijuana-cases.html.

22. Victoria Pratt (judge, Newark Municipal Court), correspondence with author, June 15, 2016. Unless otherwise indicated, all subsequent quotations are taken from this correspondence.

23. Cynthia G. Lee et al., "A Community Court Grows in Brooklyn: A Comprehensive Evaluation of the Red Hook Community Justice Center," *National Center for State Courts* (2013): 39, accessed January 18, 2017, http://www.courtinnovation.org/sites/default/files/documents/RH%20Evaluation%20Final%20Report.pdf.

24. Tom R. Tyler, *Why People Obey the Law* (New Haven, CT: Yale University Press, 1990).

25. Tom R. Tyler, "Public Mistrust of the Law: A Political Perspective," *University of Cincinnati Law Review* 66 (1998): 847–76, accessed January 18, 2017, http://digitalcommons.law.yale.edu/cgi/viewcontent.cgi?article=4035&context=fss_papers.

26. Tracey L. Meares, "The Good Cop: Knowing the Difference Between Lawful or Effective Policing and Rightful Policing—and Why It Matters," *William and Mary Law Review* 54 (2013): 1865–86, accessed January 18, 2017, http://scholarship.law.wm.edu/cgi/viewcontent.cgi?article=3487&context=wmlr; Tyler, "Public Mistrust of the Law: A Political Perspective."

27. See, for example, Robert D. Putnam, "E Pluribus Unum: Diversity and Community in the Twenty-First Century: The 2006 Johan Skytte Prize Lecture," *Scandinavian Political Studies* 30 (2007): 137–74, doi: 10.1111/j.1467-9477.2007.00176.x; Robert J. Sampson, "How Does Community Context Matter? Social Mechanisms and the Explanation of Crime Rates," in *The Explanation of Crime: Contexts, Mechanisms, and Development*, ed. Per-Olof H. Wikström and Robert J. Sampson (Cambridge: Cambridge University Press, 2006), 31–60; Jane Jacobs, *The Death and Life of Great American Cities* (New York: Random House, 1961).

28. Wally Bazemore (community activist, Red Hook), interview with author, May 2, 2016.

29. Joshua Feinzig, Chris McAllister, and Thomas Harvey, "It's Not Just Ferguson: Missouri Supreme Court Should Consolidate the Municipal Court System," ArchCity Defenders, August 14, 2015, accessed January 18, 2017, http://www.archcitydefenders.org/wp-content/uploads/2014/07/Its-Not-Just-Ferguson-Consolidate-the-Municipal-Courts.pdf.

30. Rachel Lippman, "St. Louis County Among 20 Jurisdictions Competing for Funds to Reduce Jail Populations," St. Louis Public Radio, January 6, 2016, accessed January 18, 2017, http://news.stlpublicradio.org/post/st-louis-county-among-20-jurisdictions-competing-funds-reduce-jail-populations.

31. Lee et al., "A Community Court Grows in Brooklyn," 5.

32. Ibid.

33. Alice Tapia (community resident, Red Hook), interview with author, May 3, 2016.

34. Ras Baraka, "Criminal Justice Best Practices" (White House panel discussion moderated by Angie Martinez, Washington, D.C., September 18, 2015).

4. Calculated Risks

1. *Risk Principle of Case Classification in Correctional Treatment: A Meta-Analytic Investigation*, International Journal of Offender Therapy and Comparative Criminology (2006).

2. Jeremy Travis, "Summoning the Superheroes: Harnessing Science and Passion to Create a More Effective and Humane Response to Crime: Keynote Address on the Occasion of the Twenty-Fifth Anniversary of The Sentencing Project" (speech to the National Press Club, Washington, D.C., October 11, 2011), http://johnjay.jjay.cuny.edu/extra2/presidenttravis/SentencingProjectSpeech.pdf.

3. Tim Murray (director emeritus, Pretrial Justice Institute), interview with author, August 3, 2015.

4. Christopher T. Lowenkamp, Edward J. Latessa, and Alexander M. Holsinger, "The Risk Principle in Action: What Have We Learned from 13,676 Offenders and 97 Correctional Programs?," *Crime & Delinquency* 51 (2006): 1–17.

5. Anne Milgram, "Moneyballing Criminal Justice," *The Atlantic*, June 20, 2012, accessed January 19, 2017, http://www.theatlantic.com/national/archive/2012/06/moneyballing-criminal-justice/258703.

6. Douglas S. Lipton, Robert Martinson, and Judith Wilks, *The Effectiveness of Correctional Treatment: A Survey of Treatment Evaluation Studies* (New York: Praeger, 1975).

7. See D.A. Andrews and James Bonta, "Rehabilitating Criminal Justice Policy and Practice," *Psychology, Public Policy, and Law* 16 (2010): 39–55; Lowenkamp et al., "The Risk Principle in Action"; Elizabeth K. Drake, "'What Works in Community Supervision: Interim Report," Washington State Institute for Public Policy, 2011, accessed January 19, 2017, http://www.wsipp.wa.gov/ReportFile/1094.

8. For one of the original texts on Risk-Need-Responsivity, see Don A. Andrews, "Recidivism Is Predictable and Can Be Influenced: Using Risk Assessments to Reduce Recidivism," *Forum on Corrections Research* 1 (1989): 11–17. For an update on its empirical support, see Craig Dowden and D.A. Andrews, "What Works in Young Offender Treatment: A Meta-Analysis," *Forum on Corrections Research* 11 (1999): 21–24.

9. Kelly Hannah-Moffat (criminologist, University of Toronto), interview with author, July 29, 2015. Unless otherwise indicated, all subsequent quotations are taken from this interview.

10. Lowenkamp et al., "The Risk Principle in Action."

11. Edward Latessa (criminologist, University of Cincinnati), interview with author, July 21, 2015. Unless otherwise indicated, all subsequent quotations are taken from this interview.

12. Jennifer Skeem (clinical psychologist and professor, University of California at Berkeley), interview with author, July 30, 2015. Unless

otherwise indicated, all subsequent quotations are taken from this interview.

13. Bradley Jacobs, interview with author, June 8, 2016. Jacobs has since left CASES and now serves as director of the Center for Rehabilitation and Recovery at the Coalition of Behavioral Health Agencies, Inc.

14. Joseph Margulies, "The Limits of Criminal Justice Reform," *Boston Review*, November 17, 2015, accessed January 19, 2017, https://boston review.net/us/joseph-margulies-criminal-justice-transformation.

15. Juliana Taymans (author and professor, George Washington University), correspondence with author, June 12, 2016. Unless otherwise indicated, all subsequent quotations are taken from this correspondence.

16. Mark W. Lipsey, Nana A. Landenberger, and Sandra J. Wilson, "Effects of Cognitive-Behavioral Programs for Criminal Offenders," *Campbell Systematic Reviews* 6 (2007).

17. J.C. Norcross and B.E. Wampold, "Evidence-Based Therapy Relationships: Research Conclusions and Clinical Practices," *Psychotherapy* 48 (2011): 98–102.

18. Guy Bourgon and Barbara Armstrong, "Transferring the Principles of Effective Treatment into a 'Real World' Setting," *Criminal Justice and Behavior* 32 (2005): 3–25.

19. Edward Latessa (professor and director, University of Cincinnati), interview with author, July 21, 2015.

20. Devlin Barrett, "Holder Cautions on Risk of Bias in Big Data Use in Criminal Justice," *Wall Street Journal*, August 1, 2014, accessed January 19, 2017, http://www.wsj.com/articles/u-s-attorney-gen eral-cautions-on-risk-of-bias-in-big-data-use-in-criminal-justice -1406916606.

21. Hamilton Nolan, "How We Imprison the Poor for Crimes That Haven't Happened Yet," *Gawker*, August 11, 2014, accessed January 19, 2017, http://gawker.com/how-we-imprison-the-poor-for -crimes-that-havent-happene-1619365168.

22. German Lopez, "One Popular Fix for Mass Incarceration Could Make Racial Disparities Even Worse," *Vox*, August 25, 2014, accessed January 19, 2017, http://www.vox.com/2014/8/25/5995757/evidence-based-sentencing-racism.

23. "Attorney General Eric Holder Speaks at the National Association of Criminal Defense Lawyers 57th Annual Meeting and 13th State Criminal Justice Network Conference" (remarks as prepared for delivery, Office of the Attorney General, Washington, D.C., August 1, 2014), https://www.justice.gov/opa/speech/attorney-general-eric-holder-speaks-national-association-criminal-defense-lawyers-57th.

24. For jurisdictions that have the interest and capacity to interview defendants, there are also brief assessments that predict risk based on a combination of criminal history and the current needs of the defendant (e.g., substance use, residential instability, and employment instability). Where time allows, there are also a range of lengthier instruments available to facilitate in-depth case planning and treatment matching. These include such validated assessment systems as the Level of Services Inventory (LSI-R), the Correctional Offender Management and Profiling Alternative Sanctions (COMPAS), and the Ohio Risk Assessment System (ORAS), which are in common use in the United States, Canada, Australia, and western Europe.

25. Anna Maria Barry-Jester, Ben Casselman, and Dana Goldstein, "The New Science of Sentencing: Should Prison Sentences Be Based on Crimes That Haven't Been Committed Yet?," *The Marshall Project*, August 4, 2015, accessed January 19, 2017, https://www.themarshallproject.org/2015/08/04/the-new-science-of-sentencing#.RAerGLQ1P.

26. Faye S. Taxman (criminologist, George Mason University), interview with author, August 3, 2015.

27. Glenn E. Martin, "'Risk Assessment' Cannot Solve Systemic Injustice of Prisons," *Truthout*, April 6, 2014, January 19, 2017, http://www.truth-out.org/news/item/22854-risk-assessment-cannot-solve-systemic-injustice-of-prisons.

28. Sonja B. Starr, "Sentencing, by the Numbers," *New York Times*, August 10, 2014, accessed January 19, 2017, http://www.nytimes.com/2014/08/11/opinion/sentencing-by-the-numbers.html.

29. Bernard E. Harcourt, "Risk as a Proxy for Race: The Dangers of Risk Assessment," *Federal Sentencing Reporter* 27 (2015): 237–43.

30. Mark Soler (executive director, Center for Children's Law and Policy), interview with author, June 17, 2016. Unless otherwise indicated, all subsequent quotations are taken from this interview.

31. Jessica Eaglin and Danyelle Solomon, "Reducing Racial and Ethnic Disparities in Jails: Recommendations for Local Practice," *The Brennan Center for Justice* (2015): 28, accessed January 19, 2017, https://www.brennancenter.org/sites/default/files/publications/Racial%20Disparities%20Report%20062515.pdf.

32. Sonja Starr (law professor, University of Michigan), interview with author, July 22, 2015.

33. Martin, "'Risk Assessment' Cannot Solve Systemic Injustice of Prisons."

34. In July of 2017, Travis stepped down as president of John Jay College and joined the Arnold Foundation as senior vice president for criminal justice. The Arnold Foundation has been the leading philanthropic supporter of the spread of risk assessment in the United States.

5. Risk, Release, and Rikers Island

1. *3 Days Count: Commonsense Pretrial*, Pretrial Justice Institute.

2. J. David Goodman, "Melissa Mark-Viverito, Council Speaker, Vows to Pursue New Criminal Justice Reforms," *New York Times*, February 11, 2016, accessed January 19, 2017, http://www.nytimes.com/2016/02/12/nyregion/melissa-mark-viverito-council-speaker-vows-to-pursue-new-criminal-justice-reforms.html. The Center for Court Innovation is providing research and strategic support to the commission.

3. Michael Schwirtz and Michael Winerip, "Violence by Rikers Guards Grew Under Bloomberg," *New York Times*, August 14, 2014, accessed January 20, 2017, https://www.nytimes.com/2014/08/14/nyregion /why-violence-toward-inmates-at-rikers-grew.html?_r=0.

4. "Table: Estimated Number of Persons under Correctional Supervision in the United States, 1980–2014," Bureau of Justice Statistics: Key Statistics, July 19, 2016, accessed September 12, 2016, http:// www.bjs.gov/content/keystatistics/excel/Correctional_population _counts_by_status_1980-2014.xlsx.

5. United States Attorney's Office Southern District of New York, "Manhattan U.S. Attorney Finds Pattern and Practice of Excessive Force and Violence at NYC Jails on Rikers Island That Violates the Constitutional Rights of Adolescent Male Inmates," press release, August 4, 2014, https://www.justice.gov/usao-sdny/pr /manhattan-us-attorney-finds-pattern-and-practice-excessive -force-and-violence-nyc-jails.

6. Benjamin Weiser and Michael Schwirtz, "U.S. Inquiry Finds a 'Culture of Violence' Against Teenage Inmates at Rikers Island," *New York Times*, August 4, 2014, accessed January 19, 2017, http://www .nytimes.com/2014/08/05/nyregion/us-attorneys-office-reveals -civil-rights-investigation-at-rikers-island.html?_r=0.

7. Jennifer Gonnerman, "Before the Law," *The New Yorker*, October 6, 2014, accessed January 20, 2017, http://www.newyorker .com/magazine/2014/10/06/before-the-law.

8. Michael Schwirtz and Michael Winerip, "Kalief Browder, Held at Rikers Island for 3 Years Without Trial, Commits Suicide," *New York Times*, June 8, 2015, accessed January 19, http://www.nytimes .com/2015/06/09/nyregion/kalief-browder-held-at-rikers-island -for-3-years-without-trial-commits-suicide.html.

9. C. Henrichson, J. Rinaldi, and D. Delaney, "The Price of Jails: Measuring the Taxpayer Cost of Local Incarceration," *Vera Institute of Justice* (2015): 28.

10. The Editorial Board, "Imagining a Rikers Island with No Jail," *New York Times*, February 24, 2016, accessed January 19, 2017, http://www.nytimes.com/2016/02/24/opinion/imagining-a-rikers-island-with-no-jail.html.

11. J. David Goodman, "De Blasio Says Idea of Closing Rikers Jail Complex Is Unrealistic," *New York Times*, February 16, 2016, accessed January 19, 2017, http://www.nytimes.com/2016/02/17/nyregion/de-blasio-says-idea-of-closing-rikers-jail-complex-is-unrealistic.html.

12. Ibid.

13. Sarah Trefethen and Bob Fredericks, "Bill Bratton Dismisses Viverito's Pitch to Shut Down Rikers Island," *New York Post*, February 19, 2016, accessed January 19, 2017, http://nypost.com/2016/02/19/bill-bratton-dismisses-viveritos-pitch-to-shut-down-rikers-island.

14. Jeff Mays and James Fanelli, "Council Members Vow to Fight 'Non-Starter' New Jails in Their Neighborhoods," *DNA Info*, March 31, 2016, accessed January 19, 2017, https://www.dnainfo.com/new-york/20160331/rossville/council-members-vow-fight-non-starter-new-jails-their-neighborhoods.

15. The Center for Court Innovation was part of a team of organizations that helped staff the Lippman Commission.

16. Noah Hurowitz, "Replacing Rikers Island with Local Jails Is the 'Only Solution': Commission," *DNA Info*, April 3, 2017, accessed May 25, 2017, https://www.dnainfo.com/new-york/20170403/east-elmhurst/joanathan-lippman-close-rikers-commission.

17. J. David Goodman, "Mayor Backs Plan to Close Rikers and Open Jails Elsewhere," *New York Times*, March 31, 2017, accessed May 25, 2017, https://www.nytimes.com/2017/03/31/nyregion/mayor-de-blasio-is-said-to-back-plan-to-close-jails-on-rikers-island.html.

18. Of the remainder, approximately 15 percent are individuals sentenced to one year or less of jail time and 10 percent are in jail for

other reasons (e.g., awaiting sentence after conviction or awaiting transfer to a state prison). See George V. Sweeting, letter to Melissa Mark-Viverito, City of New York Independent Budget Office, September 30, 2011, http://www.ibo.nyc.ny.us/iboreports/pretrialde tainneltrsept2011.pdf.

19. "The Price of Freedom: Bail and Pretrial Detention of Low Income Nonfelony Defendants in New York City," Human Rights Watch, 2010, accessed January 20, 2017, https://www.hrw.org/sites/default /files/reports/us1210webwcover_0.pdf.

20. Pretrial Justice Institute, "New Research Highlights Flaws and Bad Outcomes of Money Bail," press release, May 18, 2016, http://www .pretrial.org/new-research-highlights-flaws-bad-outcomes-money -bail.

21. M. Rempel, A. Kerodal, J. Spadafore, and C. Mai, "Jail in New York City: Evidence-Based Opportunities for Reform," *Center for Court Innovation* (2017).

22. George Grasso (supervising judge, Bronx County criminal court), interview with author, April 15, 2016.

23. Cherise Fanno Burdeen (chief executive officer, Pretrial Justice Institute), communication with author, March 14, 2016. Unless otherwise indicated, all subsequent quotations are taken from this communication.

24. See, for example, Charles E. Loeffler, "Does Imprisonment Alter the Life Course?," *Criminology* 51 (2013): 137–67; Christopher T. Lowenkamp, Marie VanNostrand, and Alexander Holsinger, "Investigating the Impact of Pretrial Detention on Sentencing Outcomes," Laura and John Arnold Foundation, 2013, accessed May 25, 2017, http://www.arnoldfoundation.org/wp-content/uploads/2014/02 /LJAF_Report_state-sentencing_FNL.pdf; Christopher T. Lowenkamp, Marie VanNostrand, and Alexander Holsinger, "The Hidden Costs of Pretrial Detention," Laura and John Arnold Foundation, November 2013, accessed May 25, 2017, http://www.pretrial.org

/download/research/The%20Hidden%20Costs%20of%20Pre trial%20Detention%20-%20LJAF%202013.pdf.

25. United States v. Salerno, 481 U.S. 739, 755 (1987).

26. American Bar Association, "Pretrial Release," Criminal Justice Section Standards, 3rd ed. 2007, standard 10-5.8(a), accessed June 4, 2016, http://www.americanbar.org/publications/criminal_justice _section_archive/crimjust_standards_pretrialrelease_blk.html.

27. "3 Days Count: Commonsense Pretrial," Pretrial Justice Institute, accessed January 23, 2017, http://projects.pretrial.org/3dayscount.

28. Tim Murray (director emeritus, Pretrial Justice Institute), interview with author, August 3, 2015.

29. Clifford T. Keenan (director, Pretrial Services Agency for the District of Columbia), communication with author, March 11, 2016. Unless otherwise indicated, all subsequent quotations are taken from this communication.

30. This does not include warrants for prior charges, violations, etc.

31. Clifford T. Keenan (director, Pretrial Services Agency for the District of Columbia), communication with author, May 9, 2016.

32. Clifford T. Keenan (director, Pretrial Services Agency for the District of Columbia), communication with author, March 11, 2016.

33. Tara Blair (executive officer, Kentucky Department of Pretrial Services), communication with author, March 10, 2016. Unless otherwise indicated, all subsequent quotations are taken from this communication.

34. Mark Heyerly (Project Coordinator, Kentucky Department of Pretrial Services), communication with author, June 14, 2016.

35. Herbert Bernsen (director, St. Louis County Department of Justice Services), communication with author, March 17, 2016.

36. David K. Byers (administrative director, Arizona Courts), interview with author, March 21, 2016.

37. George Gascón (district attorney, San Francisco), interview with author, January 7, 2016.

38. Juleyka Lantigua-Williams, "Can a Notorious New York City Jail Be Closed?," *The Atlantic*, April 26, 2016, accessed January 19, 2017, http://www.theatlantic.com/politics/archive/2016/04/will-rikers-island-be-closed/479790.

39. City of New York, "Mayor de Blasio Announces Citywide Rollout of $17.8 Million Bail Alternative Program," press release, April8,2016,http://www1.nyc.gov/office-of-the-mayor/news/336-16/mayor-de-blasio-citywide-rollout-17-8-million-bail-alternative-program.

40. M. Rempel, C. Fisler, A. Kerodal, J. Spadafore, S. H. Lambson, and R. Berg, "Felony Case Processing in New York City: Findings and Recommendations," *Center for Court Innovation* (2016).

41. M. Rempel et al., "Jail in New York City," 17.

42. Thomas H. Coven and Brian A. Reaves, "Pretrial Release of Felony Defendants in State Courts," Bureau of Justice Statistics, 2007, accessed January 20, 2017, http://www.bjs.gov/content/pub/pdf/prfdsc.pdf.

43. The city has created five borough-based supervised programs, each of which are administered by local nonprofit organizations that responded to a formal request for proposals from the city. The programs in Brooklyn, the Bronx, and Staten Island are operated by the Center for Court Innovation.

44. Josephine W. Hahn, "An Experiment in Bail Reform: Examining the Impact of the Brooklyn Supervised Release Program," *Center for Court Innovation* (2016): iv.

6. A Crazy Idea

1. *Annual Report on Drug Use Among Adult and Juvenile Arrestees*, National Institute of Justice (1999).

2. Not all of the defendants who test positive for drugs are substance abusers, of course, but many are. Ibid.: 1.

3. Lauren Kirchner, "Remembering the Drug Court Revolution," *Pacific Standard*, April 25, 2014, accessed January 30, 2017, https://psmag .com/remembering-the-drug-court-revolution-be13836c4be3# .umlzvasup.

4. Ibid.

5. "History: Justice Professionals Pursue a Vision," National Association of Drug Court Professionals, accessed January 30, 2017, http:// www.nadcp.org/learn/what-are-drug-courts/drug-court-history.

6. S. Rossman et al., "The Multi-Site Adult Drug Court Evaluation: Executive Summary," *Urban Institute: Justice Policy Center* (2011): 5, https://www.ncjrs.gov/pdffiles1/nij/grants/237108.pdf.

7. Emily Galvin, "How Treatment Courts Can Reduce Crime," *The Atlantic*, September 29, 2015, accessed January 30, http://www.the atlantic.com/politics/archive/2015/09/how-treatment-courts-can -reduce-crime/407704.

8. Abby Frutchey, "'Not Just Another Lost Cause': How the Justice System Saved an Addict," *The Marshall Project*, January 19, 2017, accessed January 22, 2017, https://www.themarshallproject.org/2017/01/19 /not-just-another-lost-cause#.gtkttDL6d.

9. Kim Kozlowski (project director, Syracuse Community Treatment Court), interview with author, August 12, 2016.

10. Rossman et al., "The Multi-Site Adult Drug Court Evaluation," 7.

11. Thomas P. Velardi (prosecutor, Strafford County Attorney's Office), interview with author, January 26, 2017.

12. Eric Eckholm, "Courts Give Addicts a Chance to Straighten Out," *New York Times*, October 14, 2008, accessed January 30, 2017, http:// www.nytimes.com/2008/10/15/us/15drugs.html.

13. A. Bhati, J. Roman, and Aaron Chalfin, "To Treat or Not to Treat: Evidence on the Prospect of Expanding Treatment to Drug-Involved Offenders," *Urban Institute: Justice Policy Center* (2008), accessed January 30, 2017, http://www.urban.org/research/publication/treat -or-not-treat/view/full_report.

14. Galvin, "How Treatment Courts Can Reduce Crime."

15. "America's Problem-Solving Courts: The Cost of Treatment and the Case for Reform: Executive Summary," *National Association of Criminal Defense Lawyers* (2009): 13.

16. Galvin, "How Treatment Courts Can Reduce Crime."

17. Melba V. Pearson (immediate past president, National Black Prosecutors Association), interview with author, May 25, 2016.

18. Travis Bocchino (graduate, Syracuse drug court), interview with author, September 1, 2016.

19. K. Holloway and T. Bennett, "Drug Interventions," in *What Works in Crime Prevention and Rehabilitation*, ed. D. Weisburd, D. Farrington, and C. Gill (New York: Springer, 2016), 234.

20. Alison Knopf, "SAMHSA Bans Drug Court Grantees from Ordering Participants off MAT," *Alcoholism and Drug Abuse Weekly*, February 16, 2016, accessed January 30, 2017, http://www.al coholismdrugabuseweekly.com/m-article-detail/samhsa-bans -drug-court-grantees-from-ordering-participants-off-mat.aspx; S. Friedman and K. Wagner-Goldstein, "Medication-Assisted Treatment in Drug Courts: Recommended Strategies," *Legal Action Center* (2015): http://www.courtinnovation.org/sites/default /files/documents/Medication-Assisted%20Treatment%20in%20 Drug%20Courts.pdf.

21. Jason Cherkis, "Kentucky Reforms Drug Court Rules to Let Heroin Addicts Take Prescribed Meds," *Huffington Post*, April 17, 2015, accessed January 30, 2017, http://www.huffingtonpost.com /2015/04/17/heroin-addiction-kentucky_n_7088270.html.

22. Alex Casale (coordinator, New Hampshire State Wide Drug Offender Program), interview with author, January 26, 2017. Unless indicated otherwise, all subsequent quotations are taken from this interview. Cherkis, "Kentucky Reforms Drug Court Rules to Let Heroin Addicts Take Prescribed Meds."

23. "Essential Components of Trauma-Informed Judicial Practice," Substance Abuse and Mental Health Services Administration,

accessed January 30, 2016, https://www.nasmhpd.org/sites/default/file/JudgesEssential_5%201%202013finaldraft.pdf.

24. Victoria Dexter (vice president of mental health treatment, Safe Horizon Counseling Center), interview with author, April, 5, 2016.

25. Alex Casale (New Hampshire state coordinator for the Drug Offender Program), interview with author, January 26, 2017. Unless indicated otherwise, all subsequent quotations are taken from this interview.

26. Douglas B. Marlowe, "Research Update on Adult Drug Courts," *National Association of Drug Court Professionals* (2010): 1, http://www.nadcp.org/sites/default/files/nadcp/Research%20Update%20on%20Adult%20Drug%20Courts%20-%20NADCP_1.pdf.

27. Judge Steven S. Alm (creator, Hawaii's Opportunity Probation with Enforcement), interview with author, July 27, 2016.

28. "State of the Art of HOPE Probation," Institute for Behavior and Health, Inc., 2015, 1, accessed January 30, 2017, http://www.courts.state.hi.us/docs/news_and_reports_docs/State_of_%20the_Art_of_HOPE_Probation.pdf.

29. TCR Staff, "Hawaii's HOPE Program Gets a Critical Review," *Crime Report*, November 11, 2016, accessed January 30, 2017, http://thecrimereport.org/2016/11/11/hawaiis-hope-program-gets-a-critical-review.

30. Beth Pearsall, "Replicating HOPE: Can Others Do It as Well as Hawaii?" *National Institute of Justice Journal* 273 (2014): 39, https://www.ncjrs.gov/pdffiles1/nij/244148.pdf.

31. Katherine Beckett, "The Uses and Abuses of Police Discretion: Toward Harm Reduction Policing," *Harvard Law & Policy Review* 10 (2016): 91.

32. Seema Clifasefi and Susan Collins, "LEAD Program Evaluation: Describing LEAD Case Management in Participants' Own Words," *University of Washington LEAD Evaluation Team* (2016): 11, accessed January 30, 2017, http://static1.1.sqspcdn.com/static/f/1185392/27320150/1478294794537/Specific-Aim-4-FINAL_UW-LEAD

-Evaluation-Qualitative-Report-11.1.16_updated.pdf?token=Ev9l
WVLjuR%2FR%2BfGW2B3p6SVu0X8%3D.

33. Sara Jean Green, "LEAD Program for Low-Level Drug Criminals
Sees Success," *Seattle Times*, April 8, 2015, accessed January 30, 2017,
http://www.seattletimes.com/seattle-news/crime/lead-program
-for-low-level-drug-criminals-sees-success.

34. Beckett, "The Uses and Abuses of Police Discretion"; Caroline Pres-
ton, "Don't Lock 'Em Up. Give 'Em a Chance to Quit Drugs," *New
York Times*, October 25, 2016, accessed January 30, 2017, http://
www.nytimes.com/2016/10/25/opinion/dont-lock-em-up-give
-em-a-chance-to-quit-drugs.html?_r=0.

35. Camille Pendley, "How Some Cities Are Helping Drug Offenders
Instead of Arresting Them," *Vice*, December 2, 2015, accessed January 30, 2017, http://www.vice.com/read/how-some-american-cit
ies-actually-help-drug-offenders-rather-than-arresting-them.

36. Ibid.

7. Challenging Populations

1. *Felony Defendants in Large Urban Counties, 2009—Statistical Tables*,
Bureau of Justice Statistics (2013).

2. Paula Tokar (captain, Los Angeles County Sheriff's Department),
correspondence with author, January 20, 2017.

3. Paula Tokar (captain, Los Angeles County Sheriff's Department),
correspondence with author, February 22, 2016.

4. Jackie Lacey (district attorney, Los Angeles County), interview with
author, June 17, 2016. Unless indicated otherwise, all subsequent
quotations are taken from this interview.

5. See, for example, Dana Goldstein, "How to Cut the Prison Population by 50 Percent," *The Marshall Project*, March 4, 2015, accessed
January 20, 2017, https://www.themarshallproject.org/2015/03/04
/how-to-cut-the-prison-population-by-50-percent; Leon Neyfakh,
"OK, So Who Gets to Go Free?," *Slate*, March 4, 2015, accessed

January 20, 2017, http://www.slate.com/articles/news_and_poli
tics/crime/2015/03/prison_reform_releasing_only_nonviolent_of
fenders_won_t_get_you_very_far.html.

6. See Christine A. Saum and Matthew L. Hiller, "Should Violent Offenders Be Excluded from Drug Court Participation? An Exami-
nation of the Recidivism of Violent and Nonviolent Drug Court
Participants," *Criminal Justice Review* 33 (2008): 291–307; "Alternatives to Incarceration," White House Office of National Drug
Control Policy, 2014, accessed January 20, 2017, https://www
.whitehouse.gov/ondcp/alternatives-to-incarceration.

7. Craig Dowden and D.A. Andrews, "What Works in Young Offender Treatment: A Meta-Analysis," *Forum on Corrections Research*
11 (1999): 21–24. See also the discussion of the Risk-Needs-
Responsivity model in chapter 2.

8. Katie Herman (social worker, Center for Alternative Sentencing and
Employment Services), interview with author, June 10, 2016. Unless
indicated otherwise, all subsequent quotations are taken from this
interview.

9. "Jevon," interview with author, June 6, 2016. Unless indicated otherwise, all subsequent quotations are taken from this interview.

10. Virginia Barber-Rioja (clinical instructor of psychiatry, New York
University), interview with author, June 28, 2016.

11. Ann-Marie Louison (director of Adult Behavioral Health, Center
for Alternative Sentencing and Employment Services), interview
with author, July 25, 2016.

12. Bradley Jacobs, interview with author, June 8, 2016. Jacobs worked
at CASES from 2006 to 2015, including as the Nathaniel ACT
Team Leader and co-director of Adult Behavioral Health Programs. In 2015, he became the director of the Center for Rehabilitation and Recovery at the Coalition of Behavioral Health
Agencies.

13. Anthony Shorris and Mindy Tarlow, "Preliminary Mayor's Management Report," *City of New York, Mayor Bill de Blasio* (2016): 63,

http://www1.nyc.gov/assets/operations/downloads/pdf/pmmr
2016/2016_pmmr.pdf.

14. "Cruz," interview with author, June 10, 2016. Unless indicated otherwise, all subsequent quotations are derived from this interview.

15. Loyal Miles (director of development and communications, Center for Alternative Sentencing and Employment Services), correspondence with author, May 24, 2016.

16. Ann-Marie Louison (director of adult behavioral health, Center for Alternative Sentencing and Employment Services), interview with author, July 25, 2016.

17. Joel Copperman (chief executive officer, Center for Alternative Sentencing and Employment Services), communication with author, August 8, 2016.

18. Joseph P. Morrisey, "Forensic Assertive Community Treatment: Updating the Evidence," SAMHSA's GAINS Center for Behavioral Health and Justice Transformation, 2013, accessed January 20, 2017, http://files.www.cmhnetwork.org/141801-618932.fact-fact -sheet—joe-morrissey.pdf; Gary S. Cuddeback, Joseph P. Morrissey, and Karen J. Cusack, "How Many Forensic Assertive Community Treatment Teams Do We Need?" *Psychiatric Services* 59 (2008): 205–08.

19. For a list of common cognitive-behavioral treatment programs in use in the United States, see "Cognitive-Behavioral Treatment: A Review and Discussion for Corrections Professionals," U.S. Department of Justice National Institute of Corrections, 2007, accessed January 20, 2017, http://static.nicic.gov/Library/021657.pdf.

20. See David Wilson and Mackenzie Doris, "A Quantitative Review of Structured, Group-Oriented, Cognitive-Behavioral Programs for Offenders," *Criminal Justice and Behavior* 32 (2005): 172–2014; Mark W. Lipsey, Nana A. Landenberger, and Sandra J. Wilson, "Effects of Cognitive-Behavioral Programs for Criminal Offenders," *Campbell Systematic Reviews* 6 (2007): https://bibliographie.uni -tuebingen.de/xmlui/bitstream/handle/10900/64639/1028_R

.pdf?sequence=1&isAllowed=y; Mark W. Lipsey, and Nana A. Landenberger, "Cognitive-Behavioral Interventions," in *Preventing Crime*, ed. Brandon C. Welsh and David P. Farrington (New York: Springer, 2007), 57–71.

21. Robert Hindman (clinical psychologist, Beck Institute), interview with author, June 17, 2016. Unless indicated otherwise, all subsequent quotations are taken from this interview.

22. Jack Bush, Barry Glick, and Juliana Taymans, "Thinking for a Change 4.0," U.S. Department of Justice National Institute of Corrections, 2016, accessed January 20, 2017, http://nicic.gov/library /032650.

23. Juliana Taymans (professor, George Washington University), interview with author, June 17, 2016. Unless indicated otherwise, all subsequent quotations are taken from this interview.

24. Juliana Taymans, "Thinking for a Change," in *The Encyclopedia of Corrections*, ed. Kent R. Kerley (Beverly Hills, CA: Wiley-Blackwell, forthcoming).

25. Taymans, "Thinking for a Change."

26. Christopher T. Lowenkamp, Dana Hubard, Matthew D. Makarios, Edward J. Latessa, "A Quasi-Experimental Evaluation of Thinking for a Change: A 'Real-World' Application," *Criminal Justice and Behavior* 36 (2009): 137–46.

27. Ibid.; Gayle Bickle, "An Intermediate Outcome Evaluation of the Thinking for a Change Program," Ohio Department of Rehabilitation and Correction, Bureau of Research and Evaluation, 2013.

28. Bush et al., "Thinking for a Change 4.0."

29. Holly Busby (executive chief, community services division, National Institute of Corrections), interview with author, July 25, 2016. Unless indicated otherwise, all subsequent quotations are taken from this interview.

30. Other widely used interventions that have been documented to have a positive impact include Moral Reconation Therapy and reasoning and rehabilitation. See Chris Hansen, "Cognitive-Behavioral

Interventions: Where They Came from and What They Do," *Federal Probation* 72 (2008): accessed January 20, 2017, http://www.uscourts .gov/viewer.aspx?doc=/uscourts/FederalCourts/PPS/Fedprob /2008-09/index.html.

31. Nana A Landenberger and Mark W. Lipsey, "The Positive Effects of Cognitive-Behavioral Programs for Offenders: A Meta-Analysis of Factors Associated with Effective Treatment," *Journal of Experimental Criminology* 1 (2005): 451–76.

32. "National Statistics," National Coalition Against Domestic Violence, accessed June 24, 2016, http://www.ncadv.org/learn/statistics; Jennifer Truman and Rachel Morgan, "Non-Fatal Domestic Violence, 2003–2012," Bureau of Justice Statistics, 2014, accessed January 20, 2017, http://www.bjs.gov/content/pub/pdf/ndv0312.pdf.

33. Amie Langer Zarling, Rosaura Orengo-Aguayo, and Erika Lawrence, "Violent Coercion in Intimate Relationships: Emerging Interventions," in *The Oxford Handbook of Coercive Relationship Dynamics*, ed. Thomas J. Dishion and James J. Snyder (New York: Oxford University Press, 2016), 215–30; Julia C. Babcock, Charles E. Green, and Robie Chet, "Does Batterers' Treatment Work? A Meta-Analytic Review of Domestic Violence Treatment," *Clinical Psychology Review* 23 (2004): 1023–53.

34. Sally Kreamer (deputy director, judicial district departments, Iowa Department of Corrections), interview with author, June 8, 2016. Unless indicated otherwise, all subsequent quotations are taken from this interview.

35. Amie Zarling (assistant professor, Iowa State University of Science and Technology), interview with author, June 16, 2016. Unless indicated otherwise, all subsequent quotations are taken from this interview.

36. Elaine Bales (facilitator, Achieving Change Through Value-Based Behavior), interview with author, June 20, 2016. Unless indicated otherwise, all subsequent quotations are taken from this interview.

37. A. Zarling, S. Bannon, and M. Berta (in press), "Evaluation of Acceptance and Commitment Therapy for Domestic Violence Offenders," to appear in *Psychology of Violence*.

38. Ibid.

39. Ibid.

40. Ibid.

41. Ibid.

42. Lettie Prell (director of research, Iowa Department of Corrections), correspondence with author, June 23, 2016.

43. Kim Bushey (program services director, Vermont Department of Corrections), interview with author, June 30, 2016.

44. Heather Holter (coordinator, Vermont Council on Domestic Violence), interview with author, July 1, 2016.

45. Josh Rovner, "Juvenile Life Without Parole: An Overview," *The Sentencing Project*, May 5, 2017, accessed May 25, 2017, http://www.sentencingproject.org/publications/juvenile-life-without-parole.

46. Vincent Schiraldi, Bruce Western, and Kendra Bradner, "Community Based Responses to Justice-Involved Individuals," *National Institute of Justice: New Thinking in Community Corrections Bulletin* 1 (2015): 4, https://www.ncjrs.gov/pdffiles1/nij/248900.pdf; A. Cohen et al., "When Is an Adolescent an Adult? Assessing Cognitive Control in Emotional and Nonemotional Contexts," *Psychological Science* 27 (2016): 549–62, doi: 10.1177/0956797615627625; J. Giedd et al., "Anatomical Brain Magnetic Resonance Imaging of Typically Developing Children and Adolescents," *Journal of the American Academy of Child and Adolescent Psychiatry* 48 (2009): 465–70, doi: 10.1097/CHI.0b013e31819f2715.

47. Quoted in Tim Requarth, "Neuroscience Is Changing the Debate over What Role Age Should Play in the Court," *Newsweek*, April 18, 2016, accessed May 18, 2017, http://www.newsweek.com/2016/04/29/young-brains-neuroscience-juvenile-inmates-criminal-justice-449000.html.

48. Gary Gately, "Should Young Adult Offenders Be Treated More like Juveniles?," *Juvenile Justice Information Exchange*, June 5, 2014, accessed May 25, 2017, http://jjie.org/2014/06/05/should-young -adult-offenders-be-treated-more-like-juveniles.

49. Nancy Campbell (founder and principle, Justice System Partners), correspondence with the author, May 4, 2017.

50. Alvin Cole (probation parole officer, Iowa Department of Correctional Services), interview with author, June 22, 2016. Unless indicated otherwise, all subsequent quotations are taken from this interview.

8. States of Change

1. Adam Gelb, Director, Public Safety Performance Project, Pew Charitable Trusts (2016).

2. Nathan Deal (governor, state of Georgia), correspondence with author, July 26, 2016. Unless indicated otherwise, all subsequent quotations are taken from this interview.

3. Jen Talaber Ryan (deputy chief of staff for communications, Office of Governor Nathan Deal), correspondence with author, June 7, 2016.

4. Michael P. Boggs and W. Thomas Worthy, "Criminal Justice Reform and Reinvestment in Georgia" (presentation, Criminal Justice Program of Study, Research & Advocacy, Harvard Law School, Cambridge, MA, November 11, 2015).

5. Ibid.

6. Michael P. Boggs (justice, Georgia Supreme Court), interview with author, June 6, 2016. Unless indicated otherwise, all subsequent quotations are taken from this interview.

7. Douglas B. Marlowe and Shannon M. Carey, "Research Update on Family Drug Courts," *National Association of Drug Court Professionals* (2012): 5, http://www.nadcp.org/sites/default/files/nadcp /Reseach%20Update%20on%20Family%20Drug%20Courts%20 -%20NADCP.pdf.

8. Adam Gelb (director, Public Safety Performance Project, Pew Charitable Trusts), correspondence with author, May 7, 2016.

9. Ibid.

10. Richard Oppel Jr., "States Trim Penalties and Prison Rolls, Even as Sessions Gets Tough," *New York Times*, May 18, 2017, accessed May 31, 2017, https://www.nytimes.com/2017/05/18/us/states-prisons -crime-sentences-jeff-sessions.html?_r=0.

11. Samantha Harvell et al., "Reforming Sentencing and Corrections Policy: The Experience of Justice Reinvestment Initiative States," *Urban Institute* (2016): http://www.urban.org/research/publication /reforming-sentencing-and-corrections-policy.

12. E. Ann Carson and Daniela Golinelli, "Prisoners in 2012—Advance Counts," Bureau of Justice Statistics, 2013, 8, accessed February 14, 2017, https://www.bjs.gov/content/pub/pdf/p12ac.pdf.

13. Brice Wiggins (senator, state of Mississippi), interview with author, June 22, 2016. Unless indicated otherwise, all subsequent quotations are taken from this interview.

14. "Final Report," *Mississippi Corrections and Criminal Justice Task Force* (2013): 11, accessed January 20, 2017, http://www.legislature.ms .gov/Documents/MSTaskForce_FinalReport.pdf.

15. "Mississippi's 2014 Corrections and Criminal Justice Reform: Legislation to Improve Safety, Ensure Certainty in Sentencing, and Control Corrections Costs," Pew Charitable Trusts, 2014, 7.

16. "Mississippi's 2014 Corrections and Criminal Justice Reform," Pew Charitable Trusts, May 2014, 6, accessed May 25, 2017, http://www .pewtrusts.org/~/media/assets/2014/09/pspp_mississippi_2014 _corrections_justice_reform.pdf.

17. Jody Owens II (managing attorney, Southern Poverty Law Center, Mississippi office), interview with author, June 13, 2016.

18. C.J. LeMaster, "More Opposition to HB 585," *MS News Now*, 2014, accessed February 10, 2017, http://www.msnewsnow.com /story/24999890/more-opposition-of-hb-585.

19. Andy Gipson (state representative, Mississippi Legislature), interview with author, June, 15, 2016. Unless indicated otherwise, all subsequent quotations are taken from this interview.

20. Pew Charitable Trusts, "MS Prison Drivers, Part I" (presentation, Corrections and Criminal Justice Task Force, Salt Lake City, UT, July 31, 2013).

21. Harvell et al., "Reforming Sentencing and Corrections Policy," 35.

22. Rollin Cook (executive director, Utah Department of Corrections), interview with author, June 8, 2016.

23. Pat Reavy and Sandra Yi, "Did New Program Allow Man Who Killed Officer out of Prison Early?," *Deseret News*, January 20, 2016, accessed January 20, 2017, http://www.deseretnews.com/article /865645823/Did-new-program-allow-man-who-killed-officer -out-of-prison-early.html?pg=all.

24. Pew Charitable Trusts, "Pew Applauds Utah Leaders for Sentencing and Corrections Reforms," press release, April 9, 2015, http://www .pewtrusts.org/en/about/news-room/press-releases/2015/04/09/ pew-applauds-utah-leaders-for-sentencing-and-corrections -reforms. I note that the state's population increased by approximately 20 percent in the same period.

25. Pew Charitable Trusts, "Utah Data Analysis Part 1: Prison Drivers" (presentation, Commission on Criminal and Juvenile Justice, Salt Lake City, UT, May 15, 2014).

26. Ibid.

27. Ibid.

28. Adam Gelb (director, Public Safety Performance Project, Pew Charitable Trusts), correspondence with author, May 7, 2016.

29. Matt Canham, "Republicans Embrace Prison Reform, and Their Liberal Counterparts," *Salt Lake Tribune*, March 1, 2015, accessed January 23, 2017, http://www.sltrib.com/home/2221403-155 /republicans-embrace-prison-reform-and-their.

30. Ron Gordon (executive director, Utah Commission on Criminal and Juvenile Justice), interview with author, June 6, 2016. Unless

indicated otherwise, all subsequent quotations are taken from this interview.

31. Zoë Towns (manager, Pew Charitable Trusts), interview with author, June 6, 2016. Unless indicated otherwise, all subsequent quotations are taken from this interview.

32. Roy Ockert, "State's Parole System Has Had Problems for Several Years," *Arkansas News*, August 13, 2013, accessed January 20, 2017, http://arkansasnews.com/sections/columns/news/roy-ockert /states-parole-system-has-had-problems-several-years.html; "Panel Seeks Court Order for Info on Parolee Suspected in Killing," Arkansas News, July 11, 2013, accessed January 20, 2017, http:// arkansasnews.com/sections/news/arkansas/panel-seeks-court-order -info-parolee-suspected-killing.html.

33. Shep Hyken, "Drucker Said 'Culture Eats Strategy for Breakfast' and Enterprise Rent-A-Car Proves It," *Forbes*, December 15, 2015, accessed January 23, 2017, http://www.forbes.com/sites/she phyken/2015/12/05/drucker-said-culture-eats-strategy-for-break fast-and-enterprise-rent-a-car-proves-it/#38df2ae974e0.

34. Harvell et al., "Reforming Sentencing and Corrections Policy."

35. Rollin Cook (executive director, Utah Department of Corrections), interview with author, June 8, 2016.

36. This shift has been accelerated by the current opioid crisis. Cynics (or perhaps realists?) would also suggest that government decision-makers are now adopting a more sympathetic perspective on drug abuse at precisely the moment that it becomes clear that many of the Americans abusing prescription painkillers such as oxycodone and fentanyl are white.

37. Greg Berman and Julian Adler, "Art, Science and the Challenge of Justice Reform," *Crime Report*, May 23, 2016, accessed January 13, 2017, http://thecrimereport.org/2016/05/23/art-science -and-the-challenge-of-justice-reform.

Conclusion

1. John Tharp (sheriff, Lucas County), interview with author, June 3, 2016. Unless indicated otherwise, all subsequent quotations are taken from this interview.
2. Taylor Dungjen, "Lucas County Jail Packed Beyond Capacity: Staff Strained by Inmate Overload While County Ponders New Facility," *Toledo Blade*, January 26, 2014, accessed January 20, 2017, http://www.toledoblade.com/Police-Fire/2014/01/26/Lucas-County-jail-packed-beyond-capacity.html.
3. DLR Group, "New Jail Feasibility Study Lucas County, Ohio: Presentation of System Assessment and Inmate Capacity Projections" (presentation, New Jail Feasibility Executive Committee, Lucas County, OH, April 17, 2014); Carol Contrada (commissioner, Lucas County), interview with author, June 3, 2016. Unless indicated otherwise, all subsequent quotations are taken from this interview.
4. Ibid.
5. Matthew Heyrman (director of public health and safety, Board of Lucas County Commissioners), interview with author, June 3, 2016.
6. The Editorial Board, "A Formula to Make Bail More Fair," *New York Times*, September 16, 2016, accessed January 20, 2017, http://www.nytimes.com/2016/09/17/opinion/a-formula-to-make-bail-more-fair.html?_r=0.
7. "Challenge Network: Overview," John D. and Katherine T. MacArthur Foundation, accessed January 20, 2016, http://www.safetyandjusticechallenge.org/challenge-network.
8. Nancy Fishman et al., "Greater Oklahoma City Chamber Criminal Justice Task Force: Report and Recommendations," *Vera Institute of Justice* (2016): 53, https://storage.googleapis.com/vera-web-assets/downloads/Publications/oklahoma-city-chamber-criminal-justice-task-force-report/legacy_downloads/OK-chamber-final-report.pdf.

9. Matthew Heyrman (director of public health and safety, Board of Lucas County Commissioners), interview with author, December 15, 2016.

10. Carol Contrada (commissioner, Lucas County), interview with author, December 15, 2016.

ABOUT THE AUTHORS

Greg Berman is the director of the Center for Court Innovation. He has accepted numerous awards on behalf of the Center, including the Peter F. Drucker Prize for Nonprofit Innovation. He is the author/co-author of *Trial & Error in Criminal Justice Reform, Reducing Crime, Reducing Incarceration,* and *Good Courts: The Case for Problem-Solving Justice.*

Julian Adler is the director of policy and research at the Center for Court Innovation. He was previously the director of the Red Hook Community Justice Center and the lead planner of Brooklyn Justice Initiatives. He was also part of a small planning team that launched Newark Community Solutions.

PUBLISHING IN THE PUBLIC INTEREST

Thank you for reading this book published by The New Press. The New Press is a nonprofit, public interest publisher. New Press books and authors play a crucial role in sparking conversations about the key political and social issues of our day.

We hope you enjoyed this book and that you will stay in touch with The New Press. Here are a few ways to stay up to date with our books, events, and the issues we cover:

- Sign up at www.thenewpress.com/subscribe to receive updates on New Press authors and issues and to be notified about local events
- Like us on Facebook: www.facebook.com/newpress books
- Follow us on Twitter: www.twitter.com/thenewpress

Please consider buying New Press books for yourself; for friends and family; or to donate to schools, libraries, community centers, prison libraries, and other organizations involved with the issues our authors write about.

The New Press is a 501(c)(3) nonprofit organization. You can also support our work with a tax-deductible gift by visiting www.thenewpress.com/donate.